Soft Furnishing Workshops

D0375744

Bed and Table Linen

Professional skills made easy

hamlyn

Contents

First published in Great Britain
in 2001 by
Hamlyn, an imprint of Octopus
Publishing Group Ltd
2–4 Heron Quays, London E14 4JP

Distributed in the United States
and Canada by
Sterling Publishing Co., Inc.
387 Park Avenue South,
New York, NY 10016-8810

ISBN 0 600 60233 8

A CIP catalogue record for this book
is available from the British Library

Printed and bound in China

This book first appeared as part of
The Hamlyn Book of Soft Furnishings

Introduction   6

Ideas and projects   **13**

Tablecloths and napkins   14

Fabric placemats   22

Picnic accessories   24

Bed linen   26

Decorative edging   32

Throws and bedcovers   34

Quilts and comforters   36

Patchwork and appliqué   40

Draw-string bags   48

Original lampshades   50

Practicalities   **58**

Cutting fabric and using patterns 59

Seams   60

Hems and bound edges   62

Piping and frills   65

Interfacings and interlinings   68

Holding fast   70

Decorative extras   72

Facts and figures   74

Glossary   75

Index   79

Acknowledgements   80

Metric and imperial measurements
Both metric and imperial measurements have
been given in the instructions throughout this
book. You should choose to work in either metric
or imperial, but do not mix the measurements
to ensure your projects' success.

Introduction

LINENS – for use on both tables and beds – have historically been highly prized and were handed down through generations of families, especially if these heirlooms were beautifully embroidered or very luxurious. People prefer easy-care linens nowadays, and choose fabrics that are simple to wash and press, but this does not limit the range of fabrics and finishings available for furnishing beds and tables.

Traditional lace, old cottons and linens, hand embroidery and woven check, striped and printed fabrics all make ideal bed and table coverings of one sort or another. Provided that the fabrics are practical enough for their intended purpose (bed and table linens need frequent laundering), then a wide range of designs and effects are available for you to experiment with.

Household linens

The bed is usually the largest item in the bedroom and so is the main focal point, so your choice of bed linen is a very important part of the room's decorating scheme. Duvets have revolutionized bed-making although some people still prefer the

Left *Traditionally, tables, sideboards and chests were draped with attractive pieces of linen and lace, many examples of which are still available on market stalls and in specialist shops.*

Above *Usually the largest item in the room, the bed is often the main focal point for the decorating scheme, so think carefully about the colours, patterns and textures used for the bedding.*

more traditional layered look, which involves flat sheets, blankets, comforters, quilts, bolsters and fitted bedspreads. However, in the excitement of choosing a special look for your bedroom and the bedding, do not forget that warmth is the most important factor.

Making your own table linen can be very rewarding, too, since you are creating something unique that can be made to fit in perfectly with your home's decorating scheme and that looks especially effective when you are entertaining or celebrating special occasions. Besides the decor of the room, consider the table's shape and size and the effect you want – whether it is formal or informal – before deciding on the style of tablecloth, napkins and placemats to make. Besides being decorative, tablecloths can also

be functional, protecting a polished table top when not in use, or disguising an ugly table. The layered look is very effective for tables and involves one cloth overlaid on another tablecloth with a different texture, shape or colour.

Choosing the right fabric

For any soft furnishing project, choose the fabric wisely – for its practicality and suitability, as well as for its appeal to you in terms of colour, pattern and texture. The fabric required for bed linen, tablecloths and napkins must be strong enough to withstand regular washing at high temperatures.

It must also feel good and, for minimal ironing, needs to be an easy-care fabric.

Linen and cotton are the preferred choices. Both comprise strong, practical fibres, which are either finely spun and woven into firm, smooth cloth or roughly spun and loosely woven for a softer effect. Cotton and linen can be mixed with each other or with other fibres. Linen union is a linen/cotton mix – practical, very hard-wearing and more economical than pure linen; cotton/polyester mixtures are easy-care fabrics, ideal for bed and table linens. They demand minimal ironing, but do not have the same luxurious feel of 100 per cent natural fibres.

LINEN: This strong cloth woven from flax has been popular for centuries and is arguably the king of fabrics. It is so durable that linen sheets, cloths and covers have often become heirlooms,and you can still find old, good-quality linen sheets in specialist shops or markets; it is also so fine that the best undergarments and night clothes are made from it. It can be washed frequently and at very high temperatures – it is hygienic, healthy and does not cause skin irritations. It also readily absorbs humidity, making it the ideal fibre to use for bedclothes. Since linen is stronger wet than dry, linen glass cloths are useful in the kitchen and tablecloths and napkins can be safely washed again and again.

Perhaps the only real drawback to using linen for everything, apart from its price, is that it is prone to creasing and demands time and care to keep it looking pristine.

Left *Make your own table linen to fit in perfectly with your other soft furnishings; it will look especially effective when you are entertaining.*

Below *The colour and texture of the table linen provides the starting point for creating a particular atmosphere or theme with the table setting. Start with the linen then add details in the form of flowers, ribbons, candles or coordinated glassware.*

COTTON: If linen is king, then cotton is definitely the most versatile of fabrics. Cotton plants are grown in warm climates and, once the flowers have died away, the soft hairy fibres come from the boll, a downy white casing for the seeds. Twisted and spun to a soft strong thread, the cotton is then woven on looms into cloth. It can be woven plain or in infinite pattern combinations from simple hopsack to heavy damasks.

Cotton may be knitted, felted, brushed or mercerized, and combines effortlessly with linen, wool, silk, rayon, lycra and many other synthetic fibres. There is a colour, weave and weight of cotton that is suitable for every household use – from curtains, blinds, loose covers, squabs, window seats and scatter cushions to tablecloths, bedcovers, sheets and pillows, towels, awnings and deck chairs.

Like linen, cotton is also stronger wet than dry, and can be washed extensively, making it the most popular, less costly alternative to linen for bedclothes and table linen, as well as loose covers, curtains and cushions.

Colour and pattern

One of the more fun elements of designing and decorating a room comes from choosing the mix of patterns and colours. Very often, a patterned fabric can be the starting point for a complete colour scheme in a room, the colours in the pattern providing the colour palette for paints, plain fabrics and other accessories.

There are few rules to follow, but do consider factors such as scale. Usually, you need to use smaller patterns for smaller items, as the overall effect may be lost if you only use part of the pattern in a project. Patterned fabrics almost always have pattern repeats to take into account when you are measuring and making up any item. A large repeat can be uneconomical, so consider making coordinating items for the same room to use up the fabric remnants. Small geometric prints are fairly easy to accommodate on most furnishings, as are all-over patterns. Fabrics with intricate, beautiful designs benefit most from being used

flat, and are therefore ideal for making tablecloths and bedspreads, where the true beauty of the design can be enjoyed.

Basic sheeting fabric is popular for making bed linen and tablecloths because of its wide width, but is generally plain rather than patterned – and most usually white. This provides plenty of opportunity for adding your own pattern and decoration, either all over an item or around the edges only. You can apply pattern yourself – by hand or machine – in the form of embroidery or appliqué. Experiment with developing your own patterns, picking up motifs from other elements in

Top right and right *Look around you for inspiration when it comes to planning colour and decorating schemes. Nature is just one source of ideas for colour and texture but there are many more if you really use your imagination.*

Left *Decorating plain linen with embroidery allows you to choose your own favourite themes.*

Below *Flowers are always perfect motifs for embroidering on table linen.*

a room. For example, you can trace patterns from china to use as a guide for embroidering table linen, or cut out elements from a printed fabric for use as appliqué shapes.

Above *With patchwork and appliqué you can create bold and unique designs suitable for making a covering for a table or bed. A stunning tablecloth can transform any old table into a beautiful object.*

Soft furnishing accessories

Finishing touches and small accessories can have a huge impact on a room. They are the fun element of decorating; they can give it individuality and style, and they can help to emphasize a specially chosen colour scheme. In addition, if you make them yourself, you will find they give you much lasting pleasure.

Fabric accessories are a perfect way to add dashes of colour and texture. The colour can be chosen to extend an overall decorating theme by adding a lighter or deeper tone. For a more eye-catching effect, use a dazzling contrasting colour.

Soft furnishing accessories also contrast well with the harder surfaces of wood, glass and ceramics.

Scatter cushions are obvious accessories, but why not consider more unusual items? You could make a draw-string bag in an attractive fabric to hang on a peg or at the foot of a bed (see page 48), or make an unusual lampshade (see pages 50–57). Most accessories are small and require only small pieces of fabric so they need not be costly. Thus, you could indulge in some luxurious fabrics such as silk or scraps of antique lace, or you could recycle the fabric from a favourite old garment.

Ideas and projects

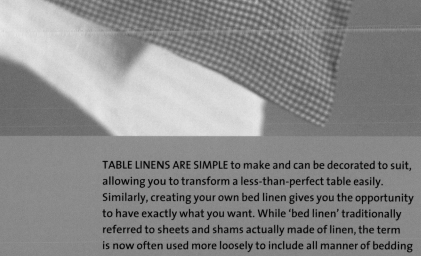

TABLE LINENS ARE SIMPLE to make and can be decorated to suit, allowing you to transform a less-than-perfect table easily. Similarly, creating your own bed linen gives you the opportunity to have exactly what you want. While 'bed linen' traditionally referred to sheets and shams actually made of linen, the term is now often used more loosely to include all manner of bedding that can be made at home – from duvet covers and pillowcases to comforters, quilts, decorative sheets and bedspreads. You will find plenty of ideas and projects on the following pages to inspire you to make your own bed and table linen, as well as accessories in the form of draw-string bags and lampshades.

Tablecloths and napkins

THE GREAT THING about tablecloths is that they can transform any table into a beautiful object. Use one as a permanent disguise for a shabby table in a bedroom or living room where it may hold a lamp and books and coordinate with curtains and other soft furnishings. Or make a fancy tablecloth for special occasions and team it with coordinating napkins and placemats for a striking dining table setting. Tablecloths, especially square or rectangular ones are easy to make and an ideal project if you are new to sewing.

Choosing fabric

Unless you want the cloth to be purely decorative, table linen fabric should be washable and in a wide width to avoid joins – sheeting fabric is ideal for this. Washable dress fabric is an alternative but it usually comes in only narrow widths, so you will have to join it. You can also use furnishing fabric for decorative cloths if you wish it to coordinate with other soft furnishings, but again you will have to join it and it is likely to need to be dry cleaned.

PVC-coated fabrics make great coverings for tables, both indoors and out, that get a lot of hard use. The added advantage is that the fabric does not fray so

Above right *Whether the setting is formal or informal, table linen brings lots of extra colour and interest, and can be made to match the room's decorative scheme.*

Right *Choose fairly absorbent and easily washable fabric for making napkins. Large tables need very wide fabric so look for wide fabrics such as sheeting to avoid the need for joins.*

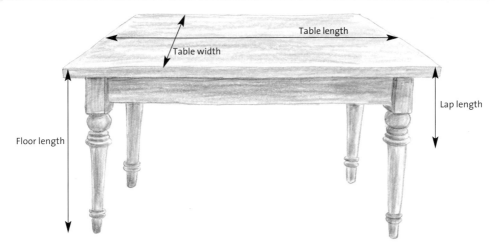

there is no need for hemming or finishing. PVC is not suitable for making napkins, but there is often coordinating non-coated fabric available from which to make these.

Measuring up

Either measure an existing tablecloth that fits your table, or measure the length and width of the table-top and then decide how long you want the cloth to be. If you want it to be lap length, sit on a chair at the table and measure from the top of the table to your lap. For a floor-length cloth, measure from the table-top to the floor. Add twice the length measurement plus 5cm (2in) for hem allowances to your table-top length and width measurements. If you want to bind the edge or add some braid around the edges you don't need to add the extra for a hem.

Napkins are usually square and can range from 30cm (12in) square for teatime napkins to 60cm (24in) square for dinner napkins – 40cm (16in) is a good compromise. Choose fairly absorbent fabric that is easily washable (cotton, gingham and seersucker are among the traditional favourites), and allow 4cm (1½in) for hems in each direction. For ideas on finishing table linen decoratively, see over.

Making tablecloths and napkins

If the fabric is not the full width of the table-cloth, you will have to join widths. Avoid a seam in the centre of the cloth, which would be very prominent and could unbalance crockery. Have a whole width of fabric in the middle of the table and sew half or whole widths on either side. Ideally, the seams should be in the overhang of the cloth. Add 1.5cm (⅝in) seam allowance to each edge where there is a seam, and use flat fell seams (see page 61) for durability. Allow extra fabric for matching large patterns (see page 59).

Once you have made any necessary joins in the fabric, turn under 12mm (½in) all round to the wrong side and then the same amount again. For napkins, turn in 1cm (⅜in) double hems. Press, then open out the corners to trim and mitre them (see page 62). To finish, topstitch by machine, close to the hemmed edge, then slipstitch the mitred corners closed.

Edging table linen decoratively

Instead of finishing tablecloths and napkins with a plain hem, you can easily decorate them with edgings and trimmings. Add a decorative touch with topstitching in contrasting coloured thread, embroidery or appliqué, or by stitching small key tassels at each corner. Equally, you could bind the edges (see pages 63–64), or add ribbon, braid, ricrac or other trimming all round (see page 72) or in one or two rows along just two edges.

Before you use any type of edging, embroidery thread or other decoration, do check that it is preshrunk, if applicable, colour-fast and washable.

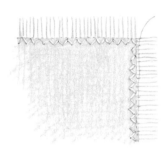

FRINGING

This is suitable for fabric with a moderately loose weave. Cut the fabric to size, then machine zigzag all around the napkin or cloth, about 2.5cm (1in) from the edge. Working on one side at a time, pull out threads around the edges until you meet the stitching. Use a pin to help you get started if necessary.

SATIN STITCH

Satin stitch can be used to emphasize a hem. Make the tablecloth or napkin as described on page 15, mitring the corners and machine topstitching close to the hem edge, then set your machine on a wide, close zigzag stitch and, using a contrasting coloured machine embroidery cotton, centre the satin stitching

Above and right *Embroidery looks stunning on white table linen. Here, the border of a shelf runner has been edged and embroidered with fruit motifs.*

produced along the hem line (see page 43). Other fancy machine embroidery stitches can be used in this way for ornamental borders.

Above *Nautical motifs have been embroidered around the sides only, allowing the cloth over the actual table-top to lie flat.*

LACE

Lace adds a delicate touch to table linen. Use broderie anglaise, cotton or nylon lace, preferably flat woven with prefinished edges. It looks much better if the corners are mitred. Make a narrow hem along the fabric edge, then machine topstitch or hand stitch the lace in position, overlapping it with the edge slightly. When you reach the corners make a diagonal pleat at 45° to allow the lace to lie flat. Machine or hand stitch along the crease then trim off any excess lace. Join the ends of lace where you started.

Blanket stitch

Blanket stitch is another decorative option for finishing the edges of heavier fabrics, and can look really good on napkin edges. If you can, turn under any raw edges first, then use the folded edge as a guide to make even stitches.

With the edge to be stitched towards you, and working from left to right, push the needle through the fabric and under the edge, so it is pointing towards you. Loop the thread over the needle, then make the next stitch about ⅛–¼in (3–6mm) further on. The looped thread should run along the fabric edge. Experiment with various embroidery yarns and threads to suit your fabric.

Bound-edged tablecloth and napkins

MEASUREMENTS

Size of tablecloth: to suit your table (see page 15)

Size of napkins: six napkins, each 40cm (16in) square

SUGGESTED FABRICS

Sheeting or washable dress fabric or furnishing fabric and coordinating cottons

MATERIALS

Fabric for tablecloth, plus 1m (1yd) of 120cm (48in) wide fabric for napkins

Contrasting fabric for binding or ready-made straight binding – enough to go round tablecloth and napkins

Scissors and sewing equipment

Matching sewing thread

With their bound edges, this tablecloth and set of matching napkins make a really impressive dining set. Take care to choose an appropriate binding that can be washed in the same way as the main fabric – some of the ready-made bindings are not colour-fast, and many are made from lightweight cottons that may not wear particularly well.

CUTTING OUT AND JOINING FABRIC

Cut a panel of fabric for the size of tablecloth required, omitting a hem allowance. Use flat fell seams (see page 61) if you need to join widths to make up the panel size required (see page 15). Cut six pieces of fabric, each 40cm (16in) square, for the

napkins. For the tablecloth, cut four strips of straight binding, each 6.5cm (2½in) wide and the same length as each side of the cloth, plus 3cm (1⅛in). (You may

Right Binding in a matching or contrasting colour adds a smartly tailored finish to napkins.

need to join fabric to get a strip long enough.) For each napkin, cut four lengths of binding, 6.5cm (2½in) wide and 43cm (17in) long.

PREPARING THE BINDING
Fold each binding strip in half lengthways, wrong sides facing inward, and press. Then turn in the long raw edges to meet along the central, pressed line.

BINDING THE OPPOSITE EDGES
Make square-bound corners by applying binding strips along two opposite edges of the fabric for the tablecloth, as described on pages 63–64. Trim the ends

of these binding strips level with the edge of the cloth.

BINDING THE REMAINING EDGES
Apply the remaining two lengths of binding for the cloth, positioning them so that they extend by 1.5cm (⅝in) either side of the cloth. Before you topstitch the binding in place, fold over the raw ends of each strip of binding so that they are enclosed when you fold the binding to the wrong side.

Above *Tartan table linen with bound edges is perfect for an elegant dining room setting.*

Oversew the corners by hand for a neat finish. (Alternatively, you could mitre the binding at the corners, if preferred, see page 64.) Follow the same instructions to bind the six napkins in the same way.

Making a round tablecloth

MEASUREMENTS

Size of tablecloth: to suit your table (see page 15 and below)

SUGGESTED FABRICS

Sheeting or washable dress fabric or furnishing fabric

MATERIALS

Fabric for tablecloth (see measuring up instructions)

Brown paper

Drawing pin, pencil and string

Scissors and sewing equipment

Matching sewing thread

Round tablecloths are often used on occasional and bedside tables, as well as on dining tables. They work particularly well when overlaid with another shorter-length round tablecloth. Since round tablecloths require a lot of fabric, you might have to join widths. As with square or rectangular tablecloths, avoid having a seam in the centre of the cloth, which is unsightly. Instead, have a whole width of fabric in the middle of the table and sew half or whole widths on either side of this central panel.

MEASURING UP

Measure the diameter of the top of your round table and then decide how long you want the tablecloth covering it to be. For a lap-length tablecloth, sit on a chair at the table and measure from the top of the table to your lap. For a long cloth measure from the edge of the table to the floor. Add twice the desired length to the diameter of the table-top, plus 2.8cm (1⅛in) for a narrow hem. Omit this if you wish to bind the edge (see pages 63–64).

Right *A pretty circular table-cloth can transform even a plain occasional table. A glass top, cut to size and its edges polished, protects the cloth from dust and dirt.*

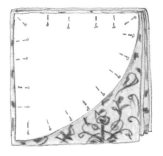

Hemming stitch

Hemming stitch gives a firm finish to the edge of a table-cloth. The stitches are sewn close together, but should not show on the fabric's right side. Working from right to left, or towards you, bring the needle out through the hem's fold and make a diagonal stitch into the fabric. Try to pick up only a single fabric thread, then stitch back under the hem. Repeat this stitch all along the length of the hem.

CUTTING OUT A SQUARE

Cut a square of fabric to these measurements. If you have to join widths of fabric, use a full-width panel at the centre, with narrower strips on either side. Fold the square in four to form a smaller square.

curve through all the layers of fabric. Open out the folded fabric to reveal a large circle of cloth.

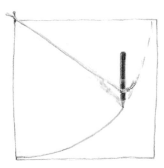

MEASURING THE CURVE

Cut a piece of brown paper to the size of the folded fabric. Using improvised compasses made from a drawing pin, a pencil and a length of string, hold the pencil upright and draw a quarter circle the radius of the finished cloth, as illustrated.

CUTTING A CIRCLE OF CLOTH

Pin the paper pattern on to the folded fabric and cut along the

FINISHING THE HEM

To finish the raw edge, neaten it with an overlock sewing machine or a standard machine zigzag stitch, then topstitch braid or fringing around the edge. Alternatively, edge the tablecloth with one continuous strip of bias binding (see page 63) or hem it with a narrow hem.

To hem the cloth, machine stitch around it, 1.5cm (⅝in) from the raw edge, then turn under the fabric edge so that the stitching is just on the wrong side. Press in place, easing the fabric as you work. Turn the raw edge under a further 6mm (¼in), press then baste in place and machine stitch close to the fold or hem by hand (see box, right).

Fabric placemats

INDIVIDUAL FABRIC PLACEMATS may be padded and quilted to offer some protection against hot dishes marking the surface beneath or they may be purely decorative on top of a tablecloth and made to coordinate with the cloth and napkins. When planning the colour and design of placemats, consider the complete table presentation – the plates, cutlery and glassware, tablecloth, napkins and napkin rings, candles and flower arrangements.

Padded placemat

MEASUREMENTS

Size of finished placemat:
40 × 28cm (16 × 11in)

SUGGESTED FABRICS

Towelling, cotton or other washable fabric

MATERIALS

Fabric for placemat (see cutting out instructions)

Iron-on fleece for wadding (see cutting out instructions)

Soft pencil or tailor's chalk

Cup or small saucer

Scissors and sewing equipment

Matching sewing thread

A 'quilted' placemat needs topstitching to secure its padding and help the mat keep its shape. The simplest form of topstitching is two parallel rows around the edge. Another option is to stitch diagonal lines at 45° to the side edges of the mat, but any design could be used. Always stitch lines in the same direction to avoid any pulling and puckering of the fabric.

CUTTING OUT, AND ADDING THE FLEECE

Cut out two pieces of fabric for the placemat, 45 × 33cm (18 × 13in). This includes 2.5cm (1in) seam allowances. (To give your mat rounded corners, mark the fabric by drawing around the outside of a cup or small saucer at each corner and cutting away the excess fabric.) Press well, as it will not be easy to iron once

Right *Crisscrossing lines of machine stitching hold the soft wadding in these placemats secure; the edges of each mat are bound with matching fabric cut on the bias.*

Far right *Unlined placemats are purely decorative, for use on a heatproof surface or with a padded tablecloth.*

the mat is made up. Cut out one piece of fleece to a similar size, but omit the seam allowance all around. Lay one piece of fabric wrong side uppermost and centre the fleece on top. Iron it in position, following the manufacturer's directions. (Use lightweight wadding instead of the fleece if preferred – see box, below.)

ENCLOSING THE FLEECE

With right sides facing, baste and stitch the two pieces of fabric together around the edges, taking a 2.5cm (1in) seam allowance and leaving a gap of about 15cm (6in) along one side. Trim any fleece from the seam allowance and trim the corners.

Turn the fabric the right side out and push out the corners neatly using the tip of a pair of scissors. Hand stitch the opening closed.

FINISHING THE MAT WITH TOPSTITCHING

For decoration and to help keep the padding in place, use large machine or hand stitches to make two parallel rows of topstitching all around the mat, 1.5cm (⅝in) and 6cm (2¼in) from the outside edge.

EATING OUTDOORS during the summer months can be great fun, and having a picnic hamper with all the colour-coordinated accessories is an added luxury for stylish alfresco eating. Consider making your own table linen just for outdoor use – choose crisp ginghams or sunny floral prints and make a tablecloth or table runner and napkins. You could use the napkins for lining a bread or fruit basket or for wrapping around cutlery, unless you make your own handy cutlery rolls...

Right *A picnic hamper can be lined with plain or quilted fabric to coordinate with other accessories.*

Cutlery roll

MEASUREMENTS

Size of four-piece cutlery roll:
30 × 25cm (12 × 10in)

SUGGESTED FABRICS

Medium-weight canvas or drill, or heavyweight furnishing cotton. Use plain, printed or colour-woven checks or stripes. Avoid large patterns because of the cutlery roll's small size

MATERIALS

Fabric for cutlery roll – 0.5m (½ yd) of 36in (90cm) wide fabric

Soft pencil or tailor's chalk

Small glass or cup

Bias binding tape – 1.65m (1⅞yd) of 2.5cm (1in) wide binding

Scissors and sewing equipment

Matching sewing thread

Individual cutlery rolls made of fabric, each with pockets to hold a knife, fork, spoon and teaspoon, are useful accessories and can be made to match plastic picnic ware as well as a tablecloth and napkins for outdoor use. The cutlery rolls are effective when lined with contrasting fabric or, if you are making a number of cutlery rolls, you could make each whole roll in a different colour.

CUTTING OUT

Cut out an outer panel measuring 30 × 25cm (12 × 10in). Cut out an inside panel to the same size in matching or contrasting fabric. Round off the corners of these two pieces by drawing around a small glass or cup to make an even curve. Cut out a cutlery insert panel measuring 30 × 12.5cm (12 × 5in) and round off the two corners along the bottom edge in the same way.

SEWING THE CUTLERY INSERT PANEL

Make a turning of ⅝in (1.5cm) along the top long edge of the insert panel and topstitch in place. Position the insert panel, right side uppermost, on the right side of the inside cutlery roll panel, matching the raw edges and curved corners. Pin together, trimming the insert panel if necessary to match the curves of the inside panel.

MAKING THE POCKETS

Using a soft pencil or tailor's chalk, mark three equally spaced vertical lines on the insert panel to form cutlery inserts. Topstitch

(1.5cm) at each end of the strip and press. Fold the binding in half lengthways so that the raw edges are enclosed and press. Topstitch close to the folded edges along the length of the binding and across the ends of the tie to stitch down all raw edges.

along these lines, stitching the insert panel to the inside panel of the cutlery roll, and reverse stitching at the neatened edge of the insert panel each time to strengthen the pockets.

ADDING THE OUTER PANEL AND BINDING THE CUTLERY ROLL

With wrong sides facing, pin together the stitched inside panel and the outer panel. Using ready-made bias binding, fold it in half lengthways and baste it in position all around the cutlery roll, enclosing the raw edges.

Turn under the raw ends of the bias binding and topstitch the binding in place (see pages 63–64).

MAKING THE CUTLERY ROLL TIE

Cut a length of bias binding, 50cm (20in) long. Turn in ⅝in

ATTACHING THE TIE

Fold the piece for the tie in half widthways and stitch the fold to the middle of one side of the cutlery roll. Insert the cutlery, roll up the fabric, wrap the tie around it and tie in a bow.

Left *Individual cutlery rolls for picnics make a lovely finishing touch and can be made to coordinate with other outdoor table linen.*

Bed linen

WITH SO MANY BEAUTIFUL ranges of bed linen in the shops it may seem that there is no need to make your own, but there are times when it makes good sense. It saves money to make your own bed linen, and it is very easy to make since it generally involves only straight seams. Also, since the bed is the most dominant part of your bedroom scheme it can be the perfect way to make sure you get the exact colours and fabrics you want. Making your own bedding also allows you to coordinate fabrics and add your own special decorative touches. While you can embellish ready-made bed linen with braid and ribbons, for example, it is much easier to do this when you make your own, especially when it comes to decorating pillowcases and duvet covers because you can conceal the raw ends of trimmings within seams.

Choosing fabric

Ordinary furnishing fabrics are not normally suitable for making bed linen because they feel too coarse next to the skin, and are suitable only for making bed-spreads, comforters or valances.

Below *Look for washable, wide-width fabric for bed linen: sheeting fabric is best as it is designed for use against the skin.*

- Pure linen is the most luxurious choice – it feels lovely and cool in summer as well as being strong and durable. To say linen will last a lifetime is not a total exaggeration, however it is

expensive, creases badly, is time-consuming to iron and not widely available.

- Pure cotton is the next choice for luxury and comfort although, unless it is 'easy care', it too needs pressing.

- Egyptian cotton is superior to ordinary cotton, having longer, finer fibres than average; percale is made from very fine threads which make a delicate, more luxurious fibre.

- Cotton flannelette has a warm, fluffy surface, which makes it particularly suitable for sheets that are to be used in winter.

- Cotton/polyester is non-shrink, hard-wearing and takes less looking after than natural fibres. It is also less expensive, but it does not have the same softness, absorbency and quality as pure cotton. Look for blends that have high proportions of cotton.

Above *Always fresh and summery looking, cotton bed linen suits the simple lines of an iron bedstead. A striking folded bedspread at the foot of the bed, adds a welcome splash of colour.*

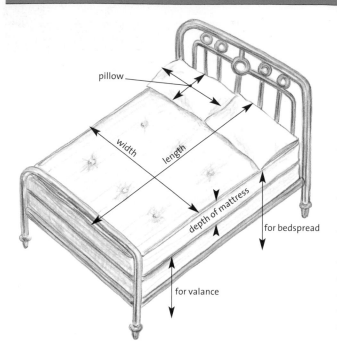

pillow

width

length

depth of mattress

for bedspread

for valance

Measuring up for bed linen

Sheeting fabric is very durable and is made extra wide to avoid having to sew any unnecessary seams. Sheeting comes in a 180cm (70in) width for single beds and 230cm (90in) for double beds. Extra-wide fabric for larger beds, 264cm (104in) and 275cm (108in) is also available but can be harder to find in stores.

To measure for a flat sheet, first measure the mattress in each direction and add extra for tuck-ins and hems. Measure the pillows from seam to seam to find the finished dimensions for the cover. Seam allowances will depend on the type of seams and opening that you choose, and whether you include a border. Duvets should also be measured from seam to seam in each direction.

Since there is such a variety of styles and sizes of beds now available, do measure up the dimensions of your bed yourself rather than assuming it is a standard size.

Making pillowcases, sheets and duvets

As these items will be washed frequently, they should be made with French seams, which

Left *Making your own bed linen, allows you to coordinate your choice of fabrics to suit your bedroom.*

Right The soft pastels of the bed linen enhance the calming effect of the room's decor and contrast well with the cast iron bed frame, creating a relaxed atmosphere.

encase the raw edges inside the item to prevent them fraying (see page 61). If you have an overlock sewing machine you can serge or overlock seam allowances. For making pillowcases and duvet covers, see pages 30–31.

Making a flat sheet

Measure the length, width and depth of the mattress. To the length and width add twice the depth plus 50cm (20in) for a single sheet and 60cm (24in) for a double sheet. Make two side turnings along the long edges towards the wrong side, first turning under 6mm (¼in) then 1cm (⅜in). Machine stitch them neatly in place. Turn the top edge 1cm (⅜in) to the wrong side, turn another 5cm (2in) then machine stitch. You can decorate this edge with machine or hand embroidery or appliqué (see page 32) if preferred. Turn the bottom edge 6mm (¼in) then 2.5cm (1in) to the wrong side and machine stitch in place.

Making a valance

Measure the length and the width of the bed, and also the height from the bed base to the floor. For the flat panel, cut out

a piece that is 3cm (1¼in) larger than the bed in each direction. For the depth of the valance side panels, add 6.5cm (2⅝in) to the height from the bed base to the floor. Cut out two panels that are 1½ times the length of the bed and two panels that are 1½ times the width. Cut and join the valance strips, using French seams (see page 61), to make a continuous loop. Along the lower edge, turn up a 2.5cm (1in) double hem and stitch this by machine. Then run lines of

gathering stitches along the top edge of the valance and draw up so that each section fits one side of the main panel. With right sides together, position the frill for the valance around the main panel, matching the corner seams of the frill with the corners of the main panel. Baste then machine stitch, taking a 1.5cm (⅝) seam allowance. Press and trim the seams, then machine zigzag stitch the raw edges to make a really durable finish.

Making a duvet cover

MEASUREMENTS

Size of duvet cover: to suit
your bed (see page 28)

SUGGESTED FABRICS

Fine cotton, cotton/polyester
or linen. Fabric must be fully
washable

MATERIALS

Fabric for duvet cover
(see cutting instructions)

Scissors and sewing equipment

Matching sewing thread

Suitable fastening, e.g. press-
stud tape, individual press studs,
small pieces of touch-and-close
fastening, fabric ties or buttons

A duvet cover is basically a large
'bag' that holds the duvet and
may be fastened at its open end
with various types of discreet
fastenings such as press studs
or touch-and-close tape. As an
alternative, you could make a
feature of the opening, and
secure it with decorative fabric
ties (see page 71) or with large
buttons and buttonholes.

MEASURING AND CUTTING OUT

Measure the length and width of
the duvet to be covered using a
cloth tape measure. Double the
length and add 15cm (6in). Add
10cm (4in) to the width and cut

out your fabric to this size. If
you have to join fabric widths
to make up the panel size, use
flat fell seams (see page 61)
and position a full width down
the centre of the cover and
strips of equal size to either side.
Decorate the cover at this point
if liked (see page 32).

NEATENING THE ENDS AND
STITCHING FRENCH SEAMS

Turn under both short ends
of the length of fabric by 1cm
(³⁄₈in) and machine stitch in
place. Fold the fabric in half,
wrong sides facing, to bring the
two hemmed edges together.

Right *Duvets originated in
Europe and have become popular
replacements for blankets and
sheets. Their covers are easily
removed for laundering.*

Stitch a French seam (see page 61) down each long side of the duvet cover.

MAKING THE OPENING

With the duvet cover now inside out and the right sides of fabric together, machine stitch for 25cm (10in) in from either side seam, parallel with the hemmed edges and 2.5cm (1in) away from them.

Above *A reversible duvet cover is made with two contrasting fabrics, which look equally good whichever side is uppermost.*

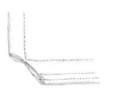

FINISHING THE COVER

Clip the corners then turn the duvet cover the right side out, using the tip of a small pair of scissors to push out the corners neatly. Stitch your chosen fastening in place in the gap (see page 70). Space whatever fastenings are used evenly – about 25cm (10in) apart – and make sure that they line up accurately opposite each other, either side of the opening. Insert the duvet and fasten the cover.

Housewife-style pillowcase

This, the most common style of pillowcase, is very straightforward to make. The cover has a flap at the back that holds the pillow in place once inserted. Cut out one back piece of fabric 3cm (1¼in) larger all around than the pillow and one front piece 3cm (1¼in) wider and 23cm (9in) longer than the pillow, placing any pattern to its best advantage.

Stitch 1.5cm (⅝in) double hems on the right-hand side of the front piece and the left-hand side of the back piece.

Pin the back and front pieces together, right sides facing, matching the three raw edges and folding the flap back. Stitch along the three sides. Clip the corners, neaten the seams and turn the pillowcase the right side out. Push out the corners neatly then press. Insert the pillow.

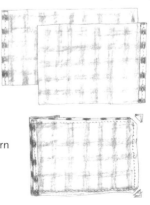

Decorative edging

BED LINEN can be personalized simply and very effectively in various ways. It is easier to do this while you are actually making the linen, but you can also add your own touch to ready-made sheets, pillowcases and duvet covers. Keep decoration to the turned-down edge of sheets and close to the open edge of pillowcases, to make them more comfortable to sleep on.

Consider decorating the edges of bed linen with a border of machine-stitched embroidery or appliquéd geometric shapes, with a trimming of lace or ribbon, or with hand-stencilled bold designs using a permanent dye. Contrasting piping along the seams of a duvet cover or pillowcases is effective, as are embroidered motifs in the corner of a plain pillowcase.

Bed linen with appliqué edging

SUGGESTED FABRICS

Sheeting fabric or dressmaking cotton/polyester – use a weight of fabric for the appliqué that is similar to the sheeting, and that has a similar fibre content. Look for fabrics that wash well, press crisply, do not fray easily, are colour-fast and preshrunk

MATERIALS

0.5m (½yd) of 90cm (36in) wide fabric in each of three contrasting colours

Tracing paper and pencil

Ready-made double sheet and two standard housewife-style pillowcases

Dressmaker's carbon paper and tracing wheel

Thin paper or card for templates

Fusible webbing (double-sided iron-on interfacing)

Scissors and sewing equipment

Matching or contrasting sewing thread

Make your bed linen unique and distinctive by adding an attractive appliqué design. The word 'appliqué' comes from the French meaning 'to apply' and involves fixing coloured fabric shapes on to a background fabric to create a bold design.

PLANNING THE DESIGN

Following the instructions on page 42, enlarge the template below to the required size and transfer it on to a piece of tracing paper. Use the tracing to check how the pattern will fit on to your pillowcases and flat sheet. The edge of the blue strip should be 3cm (1¼in) from the edge of a pillowcase, and 4cm (1½in) from the turned-down edge of a sheet (this may need to be adjusted according to seam positions). When satisfied, transfer the pattern on to the

bed linen to be appliquéd, using dressmaker's carbon paper and a tracing wheel (see box, far right).

MAKING THE TEMPLATES

Transfer the main pattern shape on to thin paper or card to make a template. Cut three or four identical templates so that you do not have to cut more if the first piece becomes bent around the edges. Mark the grain lines on the shapes as these should run in the same direction as the fabric on to which it is sewn.

Your receipt
San Diego Public Library
Mission Valley Branch

Items that you checked out

Title:
 Bed and table linen : professional skills made
 easy
ID: 31336055481221
Due: Monday, July 15, 2019

Title:
 Home from the hardware store : transform
 everyday materials into fabulous home
 furnishings
ID: 31336088958526
Due: Monday, July 15, 2019

Total items: 2
6/24/2019 10:24 AM
Checked out: 2

<><><><> <><><><> <><><><>
Renew at www.sandiegolibrary.org OR by
calling the Mission Valley Branch Library at
858-573-5007. Your library card number is
 eeded to renew borrowed items.

Left *This machine-stitched appliqué twisted rope pattern looks striking in deep blue, grey and red and gives a uniquely personal touch to a shop-bought sheet and pillowcase.*

CUTTING OUT

Back the appliqué fabric with fusible webbing. Place a template on the paper backing and draw around it on the fabric, checking the grain lines are straight. Repeat to mark sufficient shapes in each fabric colour to complete the appliqué. Cut out all the shapes. For the border edges, cut enough strips (backed with fusible webbing), 1cm (⅜in) wide, to go twice across the sheet or pillowcase.

POSITIONING AND STITCHING

Remove the paper backing from the fusible webbing and arrange the shapes in position on the bed linen. Iron in position, then stitch around the edges of the shapes, using a machine closed-up zigzag stitch (satin stitch – see page 43) or other embroidery stitch to secure them to the bed linen.

Transferring a paper pattern to fabric

Lay some dressmaker's carbon paper on the pillowcase or sheet and position the appliqué pattern on top. Use a tracing wheel to run around the outline of the pattern, so that the carbon paper marks the fabric.

Throws and bedcovers

UNLIKE A FITTED BEDSPREAD, which is made from five pieces of fabric (a top panel and four side panels), a throwover bedspread or 'throw' consists of a simple hemmed panel of fabric and is very simple and quick to make. By making your own throw you can ensure it is the right size for your bed and a perfect match to other furnishings in the room. Add finishing touches and embellishments, by quilting the fabric or adding appliqué shapes, or by edging the throw with binding, fringing or braid, as liked.

The casual look

Throws are useful in informal bedroom schemes. They may be plain or lined and quilted. They can provide an extra layer on the bed for additional warmth but are usually kept more for decorative purposes and are removed or folded down when the bed is in use. They are useful for hiding a mixture of bedding beneath, especially in dual-function rooms where you don't want the bed on show during the day.

Making a throw

Throws are generally made from a rectangle of fabric cut large enough to cover the bed from end to end and hang down the sides to the desired length. The corners can be square or rounded – make curves by drawing on the fabric around a plate. Hem the fabric with a 2.5cm (1in) double hem along all the edges. Leave the hem plain or edge it with a trimming in a contrasting texture or colour.

When measuring up for a throw, remember to allow for bedding and pillows on the bed, and decide whether the throw is to just touch or trail on the floor. If you must join fabric widths to get the required size, position a full width of fabric down the centre of the throw and use flat fell seams (see page 61) to join strips of equal size to either side. This avoids having an unsightly central seam. Allow extra fabric for matching patterns (see page 59). Any joining seams can be piped or covered with decorative braid, if liked.

Choosing fabric

Use almost any type of fabric to make a throw as long as it is crease resistant and has enough body to hang well. Since throws are not used right next to the skin, a heavier fabric can be used than for bed linen. Suitable choices include chenilles, glazed and furnishing cottons, wool mixes, dupions and kelims. White cotton lace is an attractive lightweight option and comes in extra wide widths so that seams are unnecessary. A lacy bedspread looks most effective over coloured bedding.

Left *A throw offers ample opportunity for decoration with appliqué, patchwork or machine embroidery.*

Above right *The long fringing on this heavy, textured throw is in keeping with the impressive proportions of the painted wooden bed frame.*

Right *Squares and rectangles of fabric appliquéd on to a plain background fabric and stitched with contrasting thread make a wonderfully unique throw.*

Quilts and comforters

ALTHOUGH FURNISHING FABRIC is not normally used to make bed linen such as sheets or duvet covers, it is ideal for making a comforter. It will also give a luxurious, fully coordinated look to a bedroom scheme if you use fabric from the same range as other furnishings in the room, such as wallpaper, borders or curtains.

Quilting involves sandwiching together layers of fabric and stitching in lines or around motifs on the fabric – for decoration and also to hold the fabric and wadding layers together. You can buy ready-quilted fabric, but quilting your own fabric allows you to alter the spacing and design of the quilting stitching to suit.

Making a quilted comforter

MEASUREMENTS

Size of comforter: for a standard double bed, about 50cm (20in) high plus bedding, overall quilt dimensions are about 250cm (100in) square (see box, far right)

SUGGESTED FABRICS

Lightweight furnishing fabric, such as glazed cotton

MATERIALS

Fabric for quilt – 6m (6½yd) of at least 137cm (54in) wide fabric (allow extra to match patterns)

Fabric for lining – 5m (5½yd) of 120cm (48in) wide curtain lining

Light/medium-weight polyester wadding – 7.8m (8½yd) of 90cm (36in) wide, or 5m (5½yd) of 120cm (48in) wide wadding

Large safety pins or quilting pins

Brown paper

Drawing pin, pencil and string

Scissors and sewing equipment

Matching and contrasting sewing and quilting thread

CUTTING OUT THE MAIN FABRIC

Cut out a panel of main fabric, the length of the bedspread. Check the pattern match before cutting a second panel the same length. Cut the second panel in half lengthways, and join each half width to either side of the main panel using flat fell seams (see page 61).

Cut the remaining fabric into 10cm (4in) wide bias strips, joining the strips to make a total length of bias binding of about 10.5m (11½yd) (see page 65).

THE LINING AND WADDING

Cut the length of lining fabric in half and stitch the two panels together to make a large panel the same size as the prepared main fabric panel. Cut the wadding into three (or two) equal lengths and join the panels by butting then sewing the edges together by hand with herringbone stitch (see page 69).

PREPARING THE QUILT

Lay the lining fabric out, wrong side uppermost, lay the wadding on top and then the main fabric right side up. Make sure all the edges align. Pin the three layers together randomly all across the quilt using safety or quilting pins.

Using brown paper and compasses made from a drawing pin, pencil and length of string, make a template of a quarter circle, its radius equal to the height of the bed. Hold the pencil upright and draw the

Left *Quilting around the simpler of the decorative motifs on this comforter highlights the design of the floral fabric, but straight or wavy lines of stitching are another option.*

Measuring up for a quilt

Measure the bed with all the bedclothes and pillows in position. Measure the bed's length, add to this its height from the top of the bedding to the floor. Measure the bed's width and add to that twice the height of the bed from the top of the bedding to the floor. This adds up to the amount of main fabric and plain coordinating or contrast lining needed, plus extra main fabric to bind the edges.

curve. Cut out the template, place it on the fabric and draw around it, or use the compasses directly on the quilt. Cut through all the layers of the quilt fabric, around the pencilled line, to round off the bottom two corners of the quilt.

BASTING THE LAYERS TOGETHER

Baste down the centre line of the quilt and then across the middle. Next, go across the quarter lines and the

diagonals and all around close to the edge of the quilt. Avoid basting close to where the quilting stitches will be as the machine's presser foot may get caught in the stitches. Carefully remove all the safety pins.

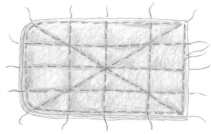

sew around the main motifs in the design, keeping the work flat. Alternatively, stitch straight lines down the quilt's length, always working in the same direction to avoid puckering.

STITCHING THE PATTERN

Fit a quilting foot to your sewing machine, select a slightly longer stitch than normal and loosen the top tension slightly. Put the sewing machine on a large table to support the weight of the quilt. If your machine has dual feed, engage it. Roll up the quilt very tightly lengthways and pull this rolled part under the sewing machine arm, so that you can work from left to right across the quilt, unrolling it gradually as you work. Using quilting thread,

BINDING THE EDGE

Press the binding strip in half lengthways, wrong sides together, then press the long raw edges in to meet along the centre line. Open out flat again. With right sides facing and raw edges level, pin the binding around the quilt edges, pinning along the binding's first fold line. Begin at one square corner of the quilt, work down one long side, along the bottom edge and up the other long side. Ease the binding around the bottom curved corners so that it lies flat,

taking care not to stretch it out of shape. Trim the binding level with the quilt edge at the top corners. Baste the binding in place close to the first pressed fold, then machine stitch along the fold. Press the binding to the wrong side along the central fold. Slipstitch the third fold of the binding in place on the back of the quilt (see pages 63–64), encasing the quilt's raw edges.

Right A quilt made in fabric from a range of coordinating furnishings that includes the wallpaper and curtains. A short frill provides extra decoration and is easily incorporated within the seams as the quilt is made up.

FINISHING THE TOP EDGE

Repeat along the top edge of the quilt, but with 1.5cm (⅝in) of binding extending on either side of the quilt. Machine stitch the binding in place, then fold in these raw ends before pressing the binding to the wrong side. Slipstitch the corners closed. Remove all visible basting.

Alternative ideas for quilting

Hand-quilting by hand is more time-consuming than machine stitching, but is much more manageable than trying to fit the quilt under a sewing machine and produces a quite different effect. Some people like to use a frame for quilting but if you baste the layers together before you quilt you can manage without one. Use neat, small running stitches for the best effect.

Consider the following ideas for alternative ways of securing the layers of fabric and wadding together. For these, measure out the positions carefully first, marking with tailor's chalk or

vanishing marker before you start sewing.

- Fabric-covered buttons (see page 71) in the same or contrasting fabric can be sewn on to the quilt through all thicknesses, at intervals. Sew them in straight lines, 20cm (8in) apart, or with every other row staggered.

- Bows of coloured embroidery cotton can be sewn through the quilt with a backstitch and tied in reef knots at intervals. Stranded silk embroidery thread can also be used as the ends fray to form attractive tassels.

Above *Warm, heavy quilts are often folded and left at the foot of the bed, for use only on very chilly nights.*

- Narrow embroidery ribbon, each length measuring about 25cm (10in) long, can be threaded through a large-eyed needle and sewn through the quilt. Tie in a small bow, trim the ends if necessary and sew the knot firmly in place with small stitches in matching cotton.

Patchwork and appliqué

YOU CAN MAKE some stunning quilts using patchwork and appliqué. Patchwork is an ideal way of recycling fabric, using remnants from other sewing projects or pieces from old clean clothes and blankets. Hand-stitched patchwork is painstaking and slow although rewarding, but machine-stitched patchwork is easier for beginners. All the seam allowances for patchwork must be the same so that the seams meet accurately each time. A binding around the edge of patchwork gives the neatest result. Patchwork and appliquéd quilts should be handwashed, never dry cleaned. (See page 32 for another project that uses appliqué.)

Right *By the nature of their size, it is much easier to make a patchwork or appliquéd quilt for a cot or single bed, rather than a double bed.*

Sun and moon cot quilt

MEASUREMENTS

Size of finished quilt: about 96cm (39in) wide × 118cm (45½in) long

SUGGESTED FABRICS

Similar weight cotton fabrics of at least 110cm (43in) wide – craft fabrics, available from needlework shops, with a tiny pattern or small texture are ideal

Safety tip

Quilts are not suitable for babies under one year old.

MATERIALS

0.5m (½yd) bright blue fabric

0.5m (½yd) navy fabric with white stars

3m (3¼yd) red and white spotted fabric

1.5m (1½yd) yellow fabric

20cm (¼yd) blue and white spotted fabric

0.5m (½yd) rusty orange fabric

20cm (¼yd) off-white fabric with grey crackle pattern

Scraps of white fabric

1.2m (1¼yd) lightweight polyester wadding

Scissors and sewing equipment

Thin card and pencil

1.5m (1½yd) fusible webbing (double-sided iron-on interfacing), at least 46cm (18in) wide

Marker pen

Sticky tape or masking tape

Machine embroidery thread in rusty orange, cherry red, white, mid-blue and dark grey

Bright blue stranded embroidery cotton

Red sewing thread

Large safety pins or quilting pins

Red quilting thread

Right *This intricate patchwork and appliqué cot quilt could make a cheerful hanging for a nursery when it has outlived its usefulness.*

For this project the shapes for the appliqué motifs are cut out first and the 12 appliqué panels (six of each design) assembled before they are joined to the plain geometric shapes to make up the patchwork. Always press the seams open as you work and, as always, use either imperial or metric measurements – do not mix them. Wash all fabrics before you start the project to avoid later shrinkage.

CUTTING OUT

To cut out the geometric fabric shapes, first cut a card template for each of the following shapes (A–J) – then draw around it on to the relevant fabric. Make sure the grain of the fabric always runs from top to bottom.

Shape	Quantity	Size
A	6	23 x 23cm (9 x 9in)
B	6	23 x 23cm (9 x 9in)
C	8	23 x 9cm (9 x 3½in)
D	9	23 x 9cm (9 x 3½in)
E	6	9 x 9cm (3½ x 3½in)
F	4	11.5 x 11.5cm (4½ x 4½in)
G	2	101 x 11.5cm (39 x 4½in)
H	2	75 x 11.5cm (31 x 4½in)
I	2	118 x 7cm (45½ x 2¾in)
J	2	96 x 7cm (39 x 2¾in)

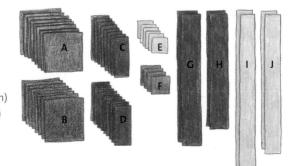

Enlarging an image

If the motif you are copying for an appliqué or embroidery project is not the right size for your use, you can easily adjust the size.

Using tracing paper and pencil, trace the item to be copied then draw a grid of 1cm (½in) squares to fit over it.

Decide on the final size of the motif you want and take another piece of paper. For a motif twice the height, draw a grid of 2cm (1in) squares (or use the appropriate size of graph paper), drawing the same number of larger squares as you had on the tracing paper; for a motif 2½ times the height of the original, make the squares 2.5cm (1¼in) in size.

Working freehand, carefully copy each part of the motif's outline, working on one square at a time, until you have a perfectly enlarged image.

PREPARING THE SUN AND MOON TEMPLATES

Enlarge the sun and moon templates given here, using a grid (see box, left) so that the sun's finished diameter is 17cm (7in) and the moon measures 16.5cm (6½in) from top to bottom. Cut templates from thin card for the sun's flame shape, the sun's centre, the moon's face, the moon's hat, plus a circle 20cm (8in) in diameter.

CUTTING OUT THE FABRIC FOR THE SUN APPLIQUÉ

Cut out six rusty orange fabric circles using the 20cm (8in) card template and back them with fusible webbing. Place the sun flame template wrong side up on the back of each circle and draw around the template on to the webbing's backing paper with pencil. Cut around the flame

shape outlines. Iron sufficient fusible webbing on to the back of the yellow fabric then cut out six sun centres from it. Trace the embroidery lines for the faces through the fabric with the marker pen. This is easier if you stick the fabric and pattern with sticky tape on a well-lit window.

CUTTING OUT THE FABRIC FOR THE MOON APPLIQUÉ

Cut out the fabric for the moon shapes in the same way, cutting six hats from the blue and white spotted fabric and six moons from the grey crackle print fabric.

ASSEMBLING THE SUN APPLIQUÉ PANELS

Remove the backing paper from each flame section of finished sun and press it in position in the centre of each bright blue square (A) using a dry iron. Using rusty orange machine embroidery thread, machine stitch around the edge of the flame shapes with satin stitch (see box, right). Near the points of the flames narrow the stitch to make turning easier. Similarly, remove the backing paper from the yellow sun faces, centre these on the flame shapes and press in place. Stitch around the shapes with orange thread, as before. Iron some fusible webbing on to the back of a scrap of white fabric and cut six mouth shapes, then iron in position. Machine embroider the eyebrows, nose and chin using the rusty orange

thread, then embroider the mouth and cheeks in cherry red. Stitch the eyes by hand with three strands of bright blue embroidery cotton using satin stitch (see page 73).

ASSEMBLING THE MOON APPLIQUÉ PANELS

Assemble the moon panels in the same way, ironing then stitching each moon face section to a navy fabric square (B) with white satin stitch, then adding the hat sections and stitching with mid-blue thread. Use a tiny scrap of white fabric for each mouth, fixing it in place with fusible webbing. Embroider the facial features by machine stitching in dark grey and cherry red.

Machine satin stitch

By reducing the stitch length when machine zigzagging, you can produce a closed-up, solid zigzag stitch, called satin stitch, which is useful for outline embroidery and appliqué. Adjust the width of the stitch for fine work.

ASSEMBLING THE PATCHWORK

Lay out the pieces for the quilt in order (see opposite). Taking 1.5cm (⅝in) seam allowances every time and using ordinary red sewing thread, machine stitch each row of sun and moon panels together with a red vertical strip (C) between each appliquéd panel. Join the rows of red strips (D) and yellow squares (E) as shown. Then join the four sun and moon strips together vertically, inserting a red and yellow strip between each.

ADDING THE EDGING STRIPS

Stitch one long red strip (G) on either long side of the suns and moons rectangle. Make up two horizontal rows using a red strip (H) in the middle and stitching a blue and white spotted square (F) on each end. Stitch these along the top and bottom edges of the rectangle.

MAKING UP THE QUILT

Cut a backing panel from the red and white spotted fabric to the same size as the finished front. Lay the backing fabric on a flat surface, wrong side uppermost, place the wadding on top and trim it to the same size as the backing fabric. Place the patchwork appliqué on top, right side uppermost. Pin all the layers together using large safety pins or quilting pins.

Baste down the middle, across the centre, along both diagonals and all around the edge close to the raw edges (see page 37). Machine with a medium-sized, straight stitch through all thicknesses along all the straight seam lines using red quilting thread (engage dual feed if your sewing machine has one).

BINDING THE SIDE EDGES

Press the long yellow binding strips (I) in half lengthways, wrong sides together, and then open out again. Stitch each of these strips along the long sides

of the quilt, working on the quilt's front, with right sides together and one raw edge and both ends of the strip level with the raw edges of quilt. Fold the strip to the back of the quilt along the pressed centre fold, press the raw edge under by 1.5cm (⅝in) along the whole length. Pin then oversew in place on the back of the quilt.

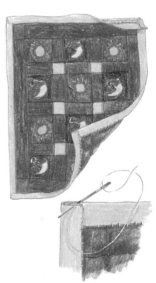

BINDING THE ENDS AND FINISHING THE CORNERS

Attach the yellow end strips (J) similarly, with 1.5cm (⅝in) extending on either side of the quilt. Fold in these 1.5cm (⅝in) overlaps to neaten the raw ends of the binding, then fold the strip to the back of the quilt, and oversew in place as before. Oversew the open corners with tiny hand stitches. Remove all visible basting.

Above *A fun day time and night time theme inspired this colourful sun and moon cot quilt.*

Appliqué techniques

Stitching appliqué by sewing machine is relatively easy. If the fabric does not fray, simply cut the shapes to size without fusible webbing and baste them in place on the main fabric. Machine stitch around the edge with a narrow zigzag stitch before going round again with a closer satin stitch (see page 43). If the fabric does fray, cut the fabric pieces slightly larger all round than the finished pattern pieces. Cut backing pieces from lightweight iron-on interfacing, omitting seam allowances. Press

the interfacing on to the back of the appliqué pieces (see page 68). Baste in place on the main fabric, then stitch all round with narrow zigzag stitch. Trim the seam allowances from the appliqué shapes close to the stitching line and stitch with satin stitch.

Use the following steps to make and apply appliqué without a sewing machine.

HAND-BACKING MOTIFS
For best results, cut the shapes 6mm (¼in) bigger all round than

the pattern. Turning in this allowance is easier if you cut the actual shape excluding the allowance in fine interfacing and press it on to the centre back of each shape. Test the interfacing first on scrap fabric as some fabrics can pucker.

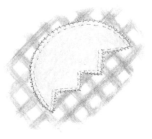

TURNING UNDER RAW EDGES

Clip curves and awkward shapes by snipping almost up to the interfacing on the back of the fabric. Turn under the allowance and press in place to the wrong side. Baste if necessary then baste the neatened appliqué shapes in position on the backing fabric.

Left A padded appliqué bed-spread is used here as an attractive tablecloth.

Right It does not matter if your stitches are not perfectly uniform for hand-sewn appliqué – they simply add to the charm of the piece and show that it is unique.

HAND STITCHING

Sew neatly around the basted appliqué shapes with tiny slipstitches or buttonhole stitch, using matching or contrasting thread, as preferred.

FINISHING

You can also topstitch close to the edge of the appliqué with some small running stitches. Use contrasting coloured thread for effect, if liked. Remove any basting stitches.

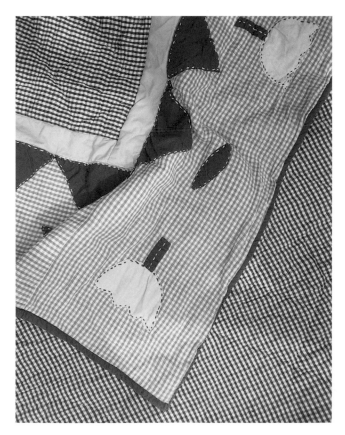

Draw-string bags

A DRAW-STRING BAG is very simple to make. In its smallest form it can be a bag of lightweight fabric to hold lavender or herbs for scenting the contents of drawers, or made from a remnant of velvet to hold precious jewellery. A medium-sized bag is ideal for keeping shoes separate from clothes in a suitcase or for carrying trainers to and from the gym. A large version is perfect for holding dirty laundry. Fabrics such as gingham and ticking stripes will give a crisp country style, while silk, velvet or damask add a more luxurious, romantic feel. Bear in mind that lightweight fabrics will draw up better than thick ones.

Laundry bag

MEASUREMENTS

Size of finished bag: 43.5 × 68cm (17 × 27in)

SUGGESTED FABRICS

Light- or medium-weight furnishing cotton or linen; striped ticking or a fabric to coordinate with room scheme

MATERIALS

Fabric for bag – 1m (1yd) of 90cm (36in) wide fabric

2m (2yd) cord for draw-strings

Scissors and sewing equipment

Matching sewing thread

CUTTING OUT

Cut out two pieces of fabric measuring 46 × 77cm (18 × 30½in). Make a 12mm (½in) cut on either side of both pieces of fabric, 14cm (5½in) from the top edge. The fabric above this point will be used as the heading.

Right *A draw-string bag can take on many guises. These robust bags, in a pretty Provençal print, are ideal for holding laundry, shoes or other items.*

PREPARING THE CASING

Make a 12mm (½in) turning to the wrong side along the top edge of one piece of the fabric and press. Turn over 12mm (½in) either side above the cuts and press.

STITCHING THE CASING

Turn the top folded edge over again so that it is level with the side cuts. Machine stitch the fabric close along this pressed edge and also 3cm (1¼in) above it to make the casing for the cord. Repeat these two steps on the other piece of fabric.

Right *A useful draw-string bag hung at the end of a child's bed becomes an attractive part of the entire room scheme when made in a coordinating fabric. This bag has been made with only one draw-string instead of two.*

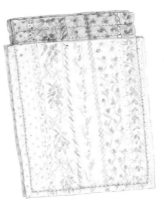

MAKING UP THE BAG

Join the fabric pieces with right sides facing and edges matching. Taking a 12mm (½in) seam allowance, stitch along the sides and bottom edge. Neaten the raw edges with machine zigzag.

THREADING THE CORDS

Turn the fabric the right side out and press the bag. To finish, thread one length of cord through from the right to the left of the front casing, then back from left to right in the back casing and tie the ends in a big knot. Feed the second cord through the casings in the opposite direction so that the knots finish up on opposite sides of the bag.

Original lampshades

LIGHTING PROVIDES the inspiration for all kinds of creative ideas as many craftsmen and makers prove. Lampshades can be sculptural and curvy, bright and bold, elegant or pretty. Apart from the practical need to provide light, all sorts of materials can be used for effect.

Shades can be made in many different sizes and shapes, and the fabric can be used flat, neatly pleated, draped, scrumpled or folded. Look for unusual fabrics such as open-weave hessian, muslin, velvet or wisps of sheer dress fabrics. They will all create wildly different effects according to their density, weave and colour. Some will filter light, while others will block it, so test out small pieces of fabric to judge the overall effect.

Home-made lampshades

There are basically two types of lampshades – soft fabric shades and firm shades, made from stiff materials such as buckram and card. Both types can easily be made at home, but you do need to take great care when making one because any defect in the workmanship of your shade will become apparent as soon as the lamp is switched on.

Try to match the line of the frame to the lamp base so that the two are in proportion and look stylish together.

Fabric and colour considerations

Consider texture, colour and quality when choosing fabric for your shade. For tailored soft fabric lampshades you need material that has plenty of elasticity; for pleated shades you need materials that drape well

Right *A subtle tassel fringe trimming around a pleated fabric shade coordinates nicely with the gingham tablecloth.*

Safety tip

With any home-made lamp-shades, for safety's sake it is advisable to use low-wattage bulbs. Try not to leave lamps on for long periods of time and consider the lamps as decorative features, rather than lights to work by. Always allow a clearance of 5–7.5cm (2–3in) on all sides of the bulb inside the shade. Whenever possible, it is best to work with natural fabrics, such as cotton, silk and wool as these tend to be less flammable than synthetic ones.

Left *A generous trimming of woven braid and looped fringing around a plain fabric-covered card lampshade suits the grand proportions of a standard lamp.*

Below *A pleated card shade is decorated with an edging of satin ribbon top and bottom and an elegant bow to match.*

such as silk, satin, lawn, broderie anglaise, chiffon and light furnishing cotton. Avoid inflammable fabrics.

Avoid large patterns and bear in mind that it can be difficult to match stripes on shaped shades. For a soft fabric shade choose the colour carefully as some colours provide a more attractive light than others. Dark colours will inhibit the light that shines through. Pale blue can cast a cold light and some greens and browns provide a dingy light, while colours such as yellow, gold, red and pink will create a cheery warmth.

Trimmings

Lampshades are ideal for decorating with trimmings. Make sure that the textures work together, matching the trimming with both the shade and the lamp base. For example, team elegant silky braids and fringes with soft silky shades, and match more coarsely woven trimmings such as cotton braid and ricrac with firm lampshades. Metallic braids, laces and velvet ribbon are all effective, too.

Measure the circumference of the shade, top and bottom, to determine the quantity of trimming required, adding an

extra 5cm (2in) to allow for turnings. Take care not to stretch the trimming being applied, although trimmings that lack elasticity, for example velvet ribbon, might need some careful stretching into position.

Some trimmings need stitching in place, others need gluing. Make sure when applying a trimming around the top and bottom edges of a shade that the two joins are opposite each other on the same side of the shade.

Stiffened silk shade

SUGGESTED FABRICS

Silk or lightweight cotton
or muslin

MATERIALS

Galvanized wire – 4.6m (5yd)
reel of 2mm (¹⁄₁₆in) gauge wire,
plus short length of fine
galvanized wire

Small pliers

Tape measure

20cm (8in) wire pendant ring

Narrow soft cotton tape or
lampshade tape

1m (1yd) silk fabric for shade

Washing-up bowl

Fabric stiffener

Rubber gloves

Scissors and sewing equipment

Sewing thread to match

Bright silk fabric arranged in
folds and creases around a
lampshade frame creates
an exotic glow.

MAKING THE FRAME

Take the 2mm (¹⁄₁₆in) gauge
galvanized wire and, using
pliers, bend it into a triangle
with each side measuring
35.5cm (14in). Make a second
triangle the same size and bind
together for strength using the
fine wire. Attach this triangle to
the pendant ring with the fine
wire. Make two more triangles
as before, this time with their
sides measuring 18cm (7in), and
bind them together. Cut three
35.5cm (14in) lengths of 2mm
(¹⁄₁₆in) wire to make the side
struts of the frame. Using fine
wire, bind the struts to the
corners of the top and bottom
triangles to complete the frame.

BINDING THE FRAME

Bind the lampshade frame
tightly with cotton tape and
hand stitch the ends together.

CUTTING OUT

To make silk bias strips, lay the
fabric on a flat surface, take one
corner and bring it across to the
selvage edge. Pin and cut the
fabric along the diagonal fold.
Cut out strips from the silk,
10cm (4in) wide, cutting parallel
to the cut edge.

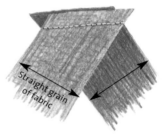

JOINING THE STRIPS

Join all the bias strips to make
one long length. Do this by
placing two strips together at
right angles each time. Have
their right sides facing and their
raw ends meeting, with a corner
of each extending to one side of
the other strip. Pin then machine
stitch from edge to edge, 12mm
(½in) from the ends. Trim the
seam allowance close to the
stitching. Reserve one bias strip
for edging the top of the frame.

STIFFENING THE FABRIC

Place the fabric in a washing-up
bowl and add fabric stiffener.
Wearing rubber gloves, spread
the liquid around with your
hands until the fabric is

Right *Richly coloured silk fabric is held in permanent folds around a tailor-made lampshade frame and creates a dramatic impact.*

saturated; remove the excess. Leave the silk to dry flat for half an hour. It should be damp enough to hold a shape.

WRAPPING THE FRAME

Take a short strip of silk and fold it in half lengthways around the top edge of the frame. Take the main strip and, working from the top downwards, wind the silk around the frame overlapping each layer as you go. Fold over the top, exposed raw edges of the strip as you work; the lower edge will be neatly hidden by the next layer of silk. Arrange the silk in folds and wrinkles.

FINISHING OFF

At the lower edge of the frame, fold under the fabric to the inside. Leave the silk to dry. When it is dry, neatly hand stitch the silk to the cotton tape along the top and bottom edges of the frame.

Re-covering an old lampshade

SUGGESTED FABRICS

Lightweight cotton, voile or other fine fabric with good draping qualities

MATERIALS

Lampshade frame, its top bound with cotton tape (see page 52)

Fabric for shade (see calculating instructions)

Soft pencil

Ribbon (optional)

Scissors and sewing equipment

Matching sewing thread

Shop-bought lampshades are easy to find in basic colours and shapes but if you want one in a special fabric, find a shape you like and re-cover the frame. You can also look for old lampshades in car boot sales or junk shops. If the cover is beyond repair, check that it can be removed. Clean the frame and spray with metal paint, if necessary.

CALCULATING THE FABRIC

To calculate the fabric required, measure the circumference of the top of the frame, then

multiply by three for full pleats. Add 2cm (¾in) extra for the seams. Measure the height of the frame and add an extra 8cm (3¼in).

PREPARING THE FABRIC

Cut out a piece of fabric to the required size. If the fabric is patterned, make sure the motifs are level. Make a double 12mm (½in) turning along one long fabric edge. Press and stitch. This is the lower edge.

Left *A simple, softly pleated lampshade is best suited to an elegant base such as this elaborate one of glass.*

NEATENING THE TOP EDGE

Along the other long edge of the piece of fabric turn over 6mm (¼in) and press. Turn again by 3cm (1¼in). Press and stitch close to the first fold.

MARKING THE PLEATS

With the wrong side of the fabric uppermost, take a soft pencil and make a mark 12mm (½in) down from the top edge and 3cm (1¼in) in from one side edge. Continue making these marks every 3cm (1¼in) along the top edge of the fabric to mark the lines for the pleats.

FOLDING THE PLEATS

To form the pleats, make a fold in the fabric at the first mark. Bring the folded edge across to the next mark. Pin in place. Form a fold at the next mark and continue in the same way to repeat the folds around the top, keeping the pleats parallel to the side edges and adjacent pleats, and at right angles to the top edge. Baste then machine stitch 2cm (¾in) from the top edge.

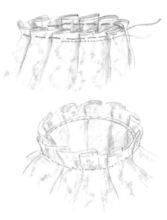

FITTING THE SHADE

Stitch together the side edges, right sides facing, taking a 12mm (½in) seam allowance. Turn the fabric right side out and slip over the frame. Attach the fabric to the cotton tape around the top edge of the frame with hand stitches following the line of machine stitching, i.e. 2cm (¾in) from the top.

Above *Patterned fabric takes on quite a different appearance when pleated. Here, the fabric has been pleated and secured along both top and bottom edges of the shade*

FINISHING THE SHADE

Make a fabric tie in matching fabric (see page 71) or use a length of ribbon and tie it around the top. Secure the ribbon to the shade with one or two hand stitches.

Fabric-covered card lampshade

SUGGESTED FABRICS

Medium-weight cotton or other suitably firm fabric

MATERIALS

Paper, pencil and ruler

Scissors

Adhesive card

Fabric for shade (see pattern instructions)

Quick-drying all-purpose adhesive

Suitable ring set or pendant fitting

DRAWING UP A PATTERN

Take a large sheet of paper, a pencil and a ruler and draw a horizontal line of a length equal to the bottom diameter of the required shade. This is line A–B. Starting at the centre of this line, draw a vertical line at right angles to it and equal to the desired shade height. Draw another horizontal line across the end of this vertical line, centred and at right angles to it,

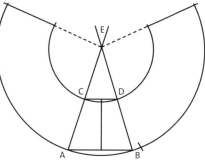

i.e. parallel to line A–B, which should be the same length as the top diameter of the shade. This is line C–D.

Draw a line from point A to join point C and extend past it.

> **Tip**
> Keep fabric-covered card lampshades clean by regular brushing with a soft brush.

Right *The bold colours of the contemporary fabric covering this card lampshade contrast with the geometric pattern on the base for an unusual look.*

Repeat from points B to D so the two angled lines cross. This will be point E.

FINISHING THE PATTERN

To draw the curved outer edge of the shade, use compasses or tie together two pencils with a piece of string that equals the distance between A and E. Using point E as the centre, draw a curved line through points A and B, and beyond. Shorten the length of string and repeat the process to draw a line through points C and D. Along the outer curved line, mark two points, the distance between which is equal to the outer circumference of the shade plus 2.5cm (1in) for an overlap. From each mark draw a straight line to point E.

USING THE TEMPLATE

Cut out the paper pattern then use it to cut out adhesive card. Use the same template to cut out the fabric for the shade, but add 12mm (½in) extra on all sides of the fabric for turnings.

COVERING THE CARD

Lay the fabric on a work surface, wrong side uppermost. Remove the backing from the adhesive card, centre it on the fabric and press it down carefully. Snip into the fabric allowance around the card and trim back to 6mm (¼in). Fold this fabric over to the wrong side and glue to the card with adhesive. Glue the two angled sides of the fabric-covered card together with a 2.5cm (1in) overlap to make the cone-shaped shade.

FINISHING OFF

Attach to the ring set or pendant fitting being used. The shade is now ready for use.

Left *Covering your own lampshade allows you more flexibility when it comes to matching and coordinating colours and accessories in your chosen decorating scheme.*

Practicalities

LEARNING SOME OF THE USEFUL sewing tips and techniques demonstrated on the following pages will ensure the success of your soft furnishing projects and give them a professional finish. There is information on sewing basics such as cutting fabric and matching patterns, stitching seams and hems, and adding fastenings. Knowing when and how to use interfacing and interlining – for stiffening fabrics and providing extra body, respectively – is useful, too. Other more decorative matters covered here include instructions for covering buttons, learning how to make piping and frills, adding decorative trimmings and working embroidery stitches.

Cutting fabric and using patterns

THE FIRST SEWING stage is to mark out cutting lines accurately, before cutting the fabric, ensuring that it stays flat as you work. When cutting rectangular panels (usually cut on the straight grain), you will get a much better finish with good-quality fabric with a straight weave.

Never use the selvage as the edge of a panel of fabric when sewing: the selvage may be tightly woven, preventing the fabric from draping naturally, and the unprinted selvage area may not be the width of the seam allowance required.

Pattern pieces

For some projects you can mark a pattern shape directly on the fabric, using tailor's chalk. Alternatively, use a paper pattern as a cutting guide – brown parcel paper is good as it does not tear easily. If you need to cut a set of matching shapes, you can ensure all the pieces are the same if you draw the shape on brown paper, cut out the paper pattern, then pin the paper pattern on to the fabric so that you can cut around it. When cutting a pattern piece, make a note of whether or not you have included a seam allowance. It is sometimes easier to add the seam allowance when you cut out, by cutting 1.5cm (⅝in)

away from the edge of the paper pattern. To cut several layers of fabric at once, pin them together to prevent them slipping (which would distort the shape of the fabric pieces). For some shapes and motifs, it is easier to mark a detailed shape on tracing paper and then transfer the pattern to the fabric using a tracing wheel and dressmaker's carbon paper (see page 33).

PATTERN MATCHING

When joining panels of patterned fabric, ensure that you match the pattern along seam lines, particularly with bold patterns on bedspreads or tablecloths. Allow a slight

margin of error when cutting out the fabric, then join the widths of fabric, as follows.

Press the seam allowance of one fabric piece under, then position it on the second piece to see the right side of both pieces to be joined. Move the folded edge over the other piece until the pattern matches. Pin the seam allowances together from beneath the fabric.

Pressing and ironing

Careful pressing is an integral part of good sewing. While ironing helps to remove fabric wrinkles and creases, pressing is a more precise technique: working on a small area at a time, you use the heat and steam from an iron to flatten details, lifting the iron up and

down. Use the point of the iron to get into corners.

Pressing your seams as you work will give you much better sewing results. After stitching a straight seam, press along the line of stitching to set the stitches into the fabric, then open out the seam and press

the seam allowance open from the wrong side. Pressing is particularly important for items such as duvet covers and pillowcases, which need turning the right side out once stitched.

(See page 73 for pressing embroidery and appliqué.)

Seams

MOST SEWING involves seams – long straight seams down square tablecloths and bed linen, short curved seams for other projects. Some seams are decorative and can be emphasized, while others need to be invisible. For strength, most seams are stitched by machine, but in some cases you may prefer to sew by hand, using a fine running stitch or backstitch.

Before machine stitching a straightforward seam, match the edges to be joined carefully, with the right sides of the fabric facing, and pin the layers together close to the stitching line. Position your pins at right angles to the stitching lines, so that the points just reach the seam line. If you prefer, baste the layers together before stitching the seam.

Flat seams

A flat seam is commonly used for joining fabric widths. To make a seam lie flat and prevent unsightly lumps on the right side of the fabric, you may need to trim and layer the seam allowance, particularly if there are several layers of fabric. If this is the case, trim each layer a different amount, so that the edges do not all fall together when the seam is pressed. Also trim, notch and clip the seam allowances of curved seams and at corners, so that when the piece is turned the right side out, you will have a smooth unpuckered curve or a crisp corner. You can also neaten the edges of a seam allowance by trimming it with pinking shears, with a zigzag or overlock stitch (see box, far right), by turning under and stitching the raw edges or, with a heavy fabric, you may prefer to bind the raw edges with bias binding (see pages 63–64).

STITCHING A FLAT SEAM

Stitch the seam with the fabric's right sides together and raw edges matching. Normally, a 1.5cm (⅝in) seam allowance is used. Reinforce the ends of the seam line by reverse stitching.

CLIPPING CORNERS

On corners, such as on a duvet cover, clip away the seam allowance diagonally across. For particularly bulky and sharply angled corners, you can taper the seam allowances further, to reduce the thickness of the fabric in the corner when the item is turned the right side out.

CLIPPING AND NOTCHING CURVED SEAMS

On an outer curve, as on a circular lined tablecloth, cut little notches out of the seam allowance every 2.5–5cm (1–2in) so that the fabric lies flat when turned the right side out. Similarly, clip into the seam allowance on inner curves so that the outer edges of the seam allowance can lie flat.

Flat fell seams

A flat fell, or run-and-fell, seam is a flat seam that encloses the fabric's raw edges without creating too much of a ridge in the fabric along the seam line. The seam is highlighted with a line of stitching running down beside it. On the back of the seam, you can see two parallel lines of stitching. It is useful for joining seams that will be under strain and for seams that may be seen from either side – on a reversible throw for example.

STITCHING A FLAT FELL SEAM

Stitch a normal seam, with the right sides of the fabric together and raw edges matching. Press the seam, press it open, then press both seam allowances to

one side. Trim the seam allowance pressed closest to the fabric to 1cm (³⁄₈in) then turn under 6mm (¼in) along the uppermost seam allowance. Pin and baste the upper seam allowance to the fabric, thus enclosing the raw edges of the lower seam allowance. Topstitch along the length of the seam close to the folded edge.

Zigzag machine stitch
One way to neaten the raw edges of seam allowances is to use a wide, long zigzag stitch – either stitching them together if the seam is to be enclosed, or stitching them separately if the seam is to be pressed open.

French seams

With a French seam, the seam allowances are closed together, but make an unsightly bulge on the fabric's reverse side. It is useful when joining fine fabrics, when making pillowcases that have to be laundered frequently, and for items such as draw-string bags, which are subject to wear on the inside as well as the outside. This type of seam is difficult to work around curves and corners. The two layers are first joined with the wrong sides together, taking only a very

narrow seam, and then the seam allowance is trimmed and the fabric turned so that you can finish the seam from the wrong side of the fabric.

STITCHING A FRENCH SEAM

Join the panels of fabric with their wrong sides together, stitching about 6mm (¼in) outside the seam line. Trim the seam allowance to 3mm (⅛in) from the first line of stitching. Press the first stitching line, pressing the seam allowances

together. Turn the fabric to bring the right sides together, folding the fabric along the first stitching line. Stitch along the seam line, thereby enclosing the fabric's raw edges.

Hems and bound edges

THE EDGES of most soft furnishings have to be carefully finished to ensure that they look good and do not fray when laundered. The options are to hem the edge or to bind it with a matching or contrasting fabric.

Hems are generally intended to provide an almost invisible finish to the edge of an item. The traditional dressmaker's hem involves a narrow turning, and then a deeper turning which can be adjusted at the final fitting stage. Most hems or edges in home sewing, however, are double hems, with two equal turnings, to give a crisper finish. Hems can be stitched in place by hand for an invisible finish, by machine using a special hemming stitch (see below) or they can be topstitched by machine.

Finishing hems

Two problem areas with hems are getting a neat finish at corners on square items, and creating a flat hem around circular items, such as round tablecloths.

To finish corners neatly, the hems have to be folded to create a diagonal pleat – a procedure known as mitring. At the same time, excess fabric is trimmed away so that the corners lie flat and are not lumpy.

The easiest way to deal with a circular hem – on a round tablecloth, for example – is to edge it with a bias strip, positioned inside the cloth, known as a faced hem. The bias strip can be eased into shape around the curved edge of the cloth. Choose a binding to match the fabric as closely as possible, or cut a bias strip from matching remnants of fabric.

MITRING A HEM

Where the hem goes around a corner, whether hand or machine stitching, reduce the fabric's bulk by mitring. First press the turning allowance and the hem all round the edge of the item to ensure the material is flat and the cut accurate.

TRIMMING THE FABRIC

Unfold the pressed fabric. Trim away the fabric across the corner, cutting 3mm (⅛in) diagonally out from the point where the innermost two fold lines cross. Then press under a 3mm (⅛in) turning across this corner.

Hemstitch

Hemstitch alternates three straight stitches with a zigzag stitch, which just catches a couple of threads of the main fabric. Press the hem in place, then fold back the fabric where the hem's fold is to be stitched to the main part of the work. Stitch along the folded hemline, catching a couple of threads of fabric as the machine needle swings to the side.

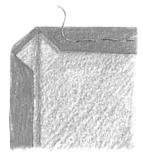

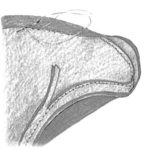

FOLDING THE MITRE

Refold the first turning of the hem, keeping the diagonal turning in place. Turn under the second fold of the hem and the edges of the diagonal turning should meet neatly at the corner. Baste in place then machine or hand stitch.

FACED HEM

Stitch the bias binding to the fabric, with right sides together and the fold line of the binding positioned just outside the fold of the item's hem. Trim the seam allowances and press. Turn the binding to the inside of the item, folding and pressing the hem in place. Slipstitch the folded edge of the binding to the wrong side of the item, keeping it flat as you stitch.

Binding edges

Ready-made bias binding comes prefolded, but if cutting bias strips yourself (see page 65), press in turnings down each long edge before sewing. The turnings should be just under half the width of the finished binding. Turn over and press. The fold lines become stitching lines when using the binding.

To bind the edge of a piece of fabric, open out one half of the binding and position it along the edge to be bound. Then stitch it, fold it over the raw edges of fabric and binding and stitch the folded edge of binding down.

You can either machine stitch the binding to the right side of the fabric, then turn it to the wrong side and slipstitch the remaining folded edge by hand, or attach the binding to the wrong side of the item, then fold it over and topstitch the folded edge in place by machine. Either way, the first stitching line should follow the seam line. Trim the seam allowances after making the first row of stitching along the binding.

STITCHING BINDING IN PLACE

Open out the binding and position it on the main fabric, with the right side of the binding facing the fabric's wrong side, and with the fold line of the binding aligned along the fabric's seam line. Machine

stitch along the fold line. Trim the seam allowances and press the stitching. Finish with topstitching (see next step).

binding in place then, working with the right side of the main fabric uppermost, topstitch the binding in place, stitching through all the layers close to the binding's inner fold lines.

HAND-STITCHED FINISH

Alternatively, stitch the binding to the fabric along the first fold line, their right sides facing. Trim the seam allowances and press.

TOPSTITCHED FINISH

Fold the binding over the raw edges to the right side of the fabric and press. Baste the

Turn the binding to the wrong side of the fabric, press again, then slipstitch it in place close to the previous stitching line.

Mitring bound corners

When binding square corners, for example around napkins, you need to mitre the binding at the corners by folding it and making a short, diagonal hand-stitched seam at the corner. Mitre each corner in turn as you reach it, rather than trying to mitre after stitching the binding in place.

FOLDING BACK THE BINDING

Fold the binding back on itself, forming a little tuck, equal in width to the finished binding, extending beyond the point where you stopped stitching.

stitch along the next edge to be bound. Take needle and thread and hand stitch a short, diagonal seam from the point where you finished stitching to the folded centre point of the binding. Continue stitching the binding in place along the next edge.

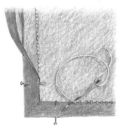

STITCHING TO MARKED POINT

Mark the corner of the main fabric where the stitching lines (seam allowances) cross. Open out the binding and, with right sides facing, machine stitch the binding to the fabric, stopping at the marked point.

STITCHING THE MITRE

Fold this extension back in a diagonal so that you can see to

FINISHING THE MITRE

Fold the binding over the edge of the fabric and stitch a second short diagonal seam across the binding before finishing the remaining edge of the binding by slipstitching in place.

Piping and frills

STRAIGHT SEAMS and hems should usually be as invisible as possible in many soft furnishings. However, you can make a feature of seams with piping and frills, outlining an item such as a quilt to emphasize its shape. Even if a pattern does not give instructions for including piping or frills and flounces, they can be fitted into almost any flat seam. Bold piping is ideal for outlining the shape of a duvet, for example, while generous frills of gathered fabric can be used to give a soft finish to bedroom pillowcases and linens.

Making piping

Piping requires strips of fabric cut on the bias, known as bias strips or bias binding. To cover piping cord, you will need 4–5cm (1½–2in) wide strips, depending on the fabric weight and the size of the piping cord to be covered. This provides for a 1.5cm (⅝in) seam allowance, plus fabric to wrap around the cord. The same strips can be used for binding edges (see pages 63–64). For large projects, such as binding the edge of a bedspread, join all the bias strips and cover lengths of piping before starting.

Piping cord is usually made of cotton and should always be preshrunk (or wash it before use) if you are inserting it in an item that is washable.

MARKING AND CUTTING BIAS STRIPS
Take a rectangle of fabric and mark a diagonal, at a 45° angle to the selvage, from one corner across to the opposite edge. Measure the width of the binding at right angles to this first line, then mark in the bias strips parallel to the first line. Cut out along the marked lines to give a number of strips.

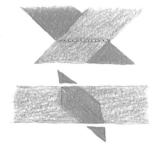

JOINING BIAS STRIPS
Position two bias strips, right sides together, at right angles, their raw edges meeting. Overlap the pieces so that their corners extend on either side and you can stitch a seam that runs from edge to edge and 1cm (⅜in) from the raw ends. Press the stitching, then press the seam open and trim away the corners. Wrap the bias strips around the piping cord, then stitch as close as possible to the cord, stitching through both layers of fabric.

STITCHING PIPING IN PLACE
Position the covered piping on the right side of one piece of the main fabric, so that the piping stitching line matches the fabric's seam line and the raw edge of the piping covering is

---

Stitching a zip or piping
Use the narrow zip/piping sewing machine foot to stitch near a zip's teeth. The foot can be adjusted to stitch on each side. The narrow foot is also used to stitch binding closely in place around piping cord or to stitch the covered cord to fabric in a seam.

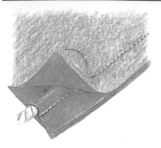

aligned with the raw edge of the fabric. Stitch in place, using a piping foot on the sewing machine (see page 65), adjusted so that the needle is between the foot and the piping cord. Then position the second panel of fabric on top of the piping, right side inward, and stitch again along the same seam.

TURNING CORNERS

Where the piping goes around the corner of an item, stitch in place as far as the corner, then snip into the seam allowance of the piping covering at the corner point, so that you can turn it around the corner. If the corner is gently curved, make several cuts into the seam allowance so that you can ease the piping into position.

JOINING ENDS OF PIPING

After pinning piping in place, cut the ends of fabric diagonally (following the fabric grain) and cut off the piping cord, leaving a 1.5cm (⅝in) seam allowance at each end. Unravel the piping cord at the overlap and entwine the loose ends together. Turn under both of the binding seam allowances and slipstitch the two pieces together.

Frills and flounces

Frills of matching or contrasting fabric can be incorporated within seams, for example around the edge of a pillowcase or a lined bedspread, or simply topstitched to a finished item, for example around the edge of a valance sheet or tablecloth.

For an inserted frill, a strip of fabric folded lengthways is usually used, which avoids the need for hemming; a topstitched frill needs its raw edges finished before you gather and stitch the frill. Decide how wide you want the frill before cutting the fabric.

PREPARING A FOLDED AND INSERTED FRILL

Cut a strip of fabric that is equal in width to twice the width of the desired finished frill, plus seam allowances. The frill length should be 1½–2 times the length of the finished seam. Neaten the frill's ends by folding the strip in half lengthways, right sides together. Stitch the short seams at each end, press, trim the allowances and turn right side out. Push out the corners using the tip of a pair of scissors then press the frill.

GATHERING THE FRILL

Gather the frill with machine stitches or sew running stitch by hand. If you are using running stitch, make two rows of stitches, quite close to each other, staggering the positions of the stitches to prevent pleats from forming. Draw up the gathers until the gathered frill length matches the length of the seam where it is to be stitched. Anchor the gathering threads around a pin at each end of the frill. Check that the fullness is evenly distributed along the frill and pin or baste it in place on the fabric panel.

SETTING IN THE FRILL

Begin by stitching the frill to the right side of one of the panels of fabric, with raw edges matching, making sure that the fullness is distributed evenly. Position the second fabric layer (for example the back of a duvet cover or pillowcase) right side facing inward, over the frill and stitch the seam. Press, trim the seam allowances and turn the fabric to the right side. Allow extra fullness at corners if the frill extends around the corner.

PIPED AND FRILLED FINISH

For extra detail, you can combine piping with a frill in a seam. Position the piping along the raw edge of the top panel, as described earlier, and stitch in place. Then position the gathered frill on top and stitch. Finally, position the back panel of fabric, so that the piping and frill are sandwiched in place. Stitch the seam. Trim all seam allowances, press and turn the fabric to the right side.

TOPSTITCHED FRILL

Cut the fabric for the frill to the width of the desired finished frill, plus a turning allowance. The length of the fabric strip should be 1½–2 times the gathered length of the frill. Turn under the hems all round and stitch, using a fine zigzag stitch or make a double hem. Gather the frill along the stitching line as before, then topstitch it in place on the fabric panel, while distributing the fullness evenly.

Tip

You might find it useful to keep tweezers handy in your sewing box ready for teasing out basting threads after stitching seams and hems. They are especially good for removing basted gathering stitches once the gathers have been machine stitched.

Interfacings and interlinings

INTERFACINGS AND INTERLININGS give home sewing a professional finish. Although many types are meant for dressmaking and tailoring, some are used to improve a finished project by adding extra hidden layers as you make up the item. Interfacings stiffen fabrics and give a crisp finish, while interlinings are soft fabrics that give extra body to soft furnishings.

Choosing and using interfacings

Interfacings come in different weights and are ideal both for stiffening fabrics and giving extra weight to home furnishing accessories. The traditional interfacings are woven, but modern non-woven ones are easier to work with as they have no grain, and so do not have to be aligned with the fabric to match the weave. Some non-woven interfacings have a special backing so that they can be ironed on to the main fabric. The interfacing is usually trimmed away close to the stitching before finishing the project, in order to reduce the seam bulk.

Buckram is a traditional, very stiff interfacing, which can be used for making lampshades. For appliqué or embroidery, use lightweight fabrics such as silk organdie, marquisette, bastiste or fine lawn interfacings to back the main fabric. Delicate fabrics hold their shape, if backed with a lightweight iron-on interfacing, and double-sided iron-on interfacing makes appliqué projects easier.

USING IRON-ON INTERFACING
Press fabric to be faced carefully before fusing the interfacing. Apply it to the fabric's wrong side. To protect the sole plate of

the iron and to ensure that the iron does not over-heat the fusible (iron-on) interfacing, use a pressing cloth between the iron and the interfacing.

APPLYING LIGHTWEIGHT SEW-IN INTERFACING
Cut the interfacing to the same size as the main fabric piece to be faced, and baste it to the wrong side. Use the two fabric layers as though they were a single layer. Trim away all the interfacing from the seam allowances, close to the seam line, after finishing the seam.

What's beneath the fabric?
When stitching appliqué to fine fabric, iron non-woven interfacing to the wrong side of the fabric motif. Do not cut out the motif.

Stabilize the main fabric by basting interfacing to the back if required. Pin the motif in place, machine stitch around the outline (see page 43) then trim away excess fabric. On the back of the fabric, remove the basting and trim the interfacing close to the stitching.

Interlinings

Interlinings are soft fabrics that are used to give extra body to soft furnishings. Traditional interlinings include bump and domette, that are used under decorative, lined tablecloths. Flannelette and synthetic forms of wadding (also available with iron-on backing for quilted projects) can be used. When choosing an interlining, check whether it will wash (or dry clean) with the fabric with which it is being used.

USING INTERLINING

Interlining is a bulky fabric, so join widths by machine with lapped seams or by hand with herringbone stitch to prevent stiffness at the join. Once the item is made up, the interlining is enclosed by the main fabric and lining, so its raw edges are protected from fraying.

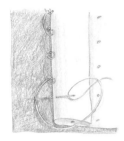

LOCKING IN INTERLINING

To prevent interlining slipping around inside between layers of fabric, for example if you are making a heavy, lined tablecloth, lock it to the wrong side of the main fabric before making up the cloth. Lockstitch is a long, looped stitch, worked down the length of the fabric on a fold in the interlining. Pick up only a single thread of the main fabric and do not pull the thread taut.

JOINING INTERLINING OR WADDING

To join layers of wadding or interlining with minimal bulk, use a wide or multi-zigzag stitch. Overlap the seam allowances, machine stitch with zigzag and then trim away the excess fabric. For bulky layers of wadding or very thick interlining, butt together the edges that are to be joined, and stitch by hand with herringbone stitch, taking stitches across the join on alternate sides.

Herringbone stitch

Herringbone stitch is both a decorative stitch and a useful one for a firm hem where you want a minimal bulk, for example with very thick fabrics. Do not make an extra fold in the hem – simply neaten the fabric's raw edge with machine zigzag stitch (see page 61) before making a herringbone-stitch hem.

Working from left to right (right to left for left-handers), bring the needle up through the hem, then insert it in the main fabric diagonally up to the right. Take a tiny stitch in the main fabric, then move the needle down diagonally to the right and take a stitch right through the hem. Repeat this stitch along the hem.

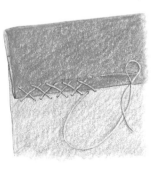

Holding fast

MANY SOFT FURNISHINGS, for example duvet covers, need openings so that they can be easily removed and cleaned. These openings need fastenings to keep them closed while in use, for example fastening by the length, zips, hooks and eyes, press studs and buttons. Many linens are finished with stylish buttons or fabric ties, but for duvet covers you may prefer to use lightweight zips or some light, plastic press-stud tape.

Fastening by the length

Nylon touch-and-close fastening comes in long strips made up of a double layer: one half has tiny hooks and the other a soft mesh of nylon loops. When joining two fabric pieces, allow an overlap equal to the width of the fastening you are using. Also allow for turning under each of the edges to be joined. Topstitch the fastening in place to the wrong side of the overlap and the right side of the underlap.

Fix lightly with glue before stitching them, as the backing is very difficult to pin in place. Use the mesh of loops on the overlap and the crisper hooks on the underlap.

Position hook-and-eye and press-stud tapes in the seam allowance or along an overlap. The eyes of the hook-and-eye tape, and the sockets of the press-stud tape, should be on the right side of the underlap; the hooks and the studs should be on the underside of the overlap. Topstitch in place. Do not stitch close to the metal or plastic inserts in the tapes.

Hand-sewn fastenings

Individual hooks and eyes, and press studs are sewn on by hand; and buttons are best sewn by hand for a secure finish. Mark the position of these closures carefully, and check both halves are aligned accurately before stitching in place.

Buttonholes and loops

Buttonholes can be stitched by machine (see your sewing machine manual for detailed instructions for making buttonholes), and hand-stitched button loops are another option. Rather more elaborate to make are rouleau button loops, created from a long fabric tube, which is stitched into loops down the overlapping edge of a closure. These can be spaced apart on the soft furnishing item or butted closely together for a rather more dramatic effect. The loops have to be set into a seam down the opening edge of the item, created by a facing of fabric.

MACHINE-STITCHED BUTTONHOLES

Buttonholes are best worked through more than one layer of fabric, so allow a generous turning on the overlapping edge where you wish the buttonhole to be. Measure the button's diameter and mark the position and length of the buttonhole on the fabric. Use the settings on your sewing machine (some are automatic) to work the outline of the buttonhole. Use fine embroidery scissors to cut the fabric between the stitches, without cutting into them.

ROULEAU LOOPS

Made from long strips of fabric, each rouleau loop should be long enough to go over the button's diameter, and have seam allowances to stitch into the opening's edge. Work out each loop's length, including allowances, and cut a strip of fabric the total length required, about 2.5cm (1in) wide.

ATTACHING ROULEAU LOOPS

Set the rouleau loops into a faced opening, so that the raw loop ends are enclosed. Position the loops next to each other for a traditional 'buttoned dress' finish, or space them apart down the opening for less work! Pin the loops along the raw edge on the right side of the overlap, with raw edges matching. Stitch in place, then position the facing

Turn under 6mm (¼in) down each long edge, then fold in half, right sides outward. Stitch the length to enclose the raw edges.

over the loops, right side down, and stitch the seam. Press, turn the facing to the inside and press again.

Fabric-covered buttons

Covered buttons provide a subtle finish to any buttoned opening. Cover button forms with fabric to match the item you are making, or add plain fabric-covered buttons to a patterned item.

Button forms are available from haberdashery departments in a range of sizes, complete with instructions. If you are

using very fine or slippery fabric, use iron-on interfacing (see page 68) to give the fabric a firmer finish before covering the button.

COVERING A BUTTON

Simply cut a circle of fabric a little larger than the diameter of the button (you will find precise instructions with the button

form) and tuck it over the front portion of the button before fixing the button back in place.

Fabric ties

Fabric ties (made in the same way as rouleau loops, see above, or as below) are simple decorative fastenings used, for example, to close duvet covers. They require very little fabric.

MAKING TIES

Cut each half of tie at least 25cm (10in) long, or make a double length to attach to an edge or insert in a seam – 10cm (4in) is a

good width. Fold the strip in half lengthways, right sides facing, and run some tape or cord along the length, close to the fold. Stitch across one end, catching the end of the tape into the seam. Then stitch along the long edge of the tie, taking a 1.5cm (⅝in) seam allowance and taking care not to catch the tape. Trim the seam allowance then pull the tape so as to turn the tie

fabric the right side out. Trim away the tape, then turn under the raw ends and slipstitch the opening closed.

Decorative extras

THERE ARE MANY different braids, fringing, cords and ribbons available for adding detail to soft furnishings without having to make custom-made piping and frills. A look round a haberdashery department will give you many ideas for ready-made finishes. Some are made for setting into seams in the fabric, for example silky, rope-twist insertion cord, which has a flange woven into it; others are topstitched in place before making up an item, for example braids and fringing on table linen, ribbon or a frill of broderie anglaise on bed linen.

Topstitched finishes

When applying a topstitched finish, such as braid, fringing, ribbon or lace, it is important to measure and mark accurately. The decoration should be applied before making up an item such as a pillowcase. This makes it easier to work and, where the trimming runs to the edge of the pillowcase, the raw edges will be stitched into the seam as you make it up.

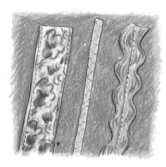

MARKING THE POSITION

Mark the trimming's position on the fabric with tailor's chalk. Decide whether to align the trimming centrally, or to one side of the marked line. Cut lengths of braid, lace or ribbon to match the marked line, allowing at least 12mm (½in) for turning under at each end.

TOPSTITCHING

Pin and baste the trimming in place, then topstitch it by machine. Wide trimmings should be topstitched close to each edge with straight stitching, or use a narrow zigzag worked over the trimming's edge. If you are making two lines of stitching, work them both in the same direction to avoid twisting and distorting the trimming. Extremely narrow trimmings can be held in place with a single line of straight or zigzag stitching along the trimming's centre.

TURNING A CORNER

On bed and table linen, you may want to add a square or rectangle of ribbon or braid, topstitched in place, which involves mitring the corners. Mark the outer line of the rectangle as a guide for positioning the trimming. Topstitch the trimming in place along the outer edge, stopping at the corner. Reverse stitch to strengthen the stitching, then remove the fabric panel from the sewing machine. Fold the trimming back on itself at the corner and machine stitch a short, diagonal seam across the trimming, from the outer corner down to the trimming's inner edge, as shown. Clip away the seam allowance, if necessary. Press flat, then continue stitching to the next corner. When complete, topstitch the inner edge of the trimming in place.

Embroidery

Embroidered details – perhaps a floral motif on table linen or pillowcases, or an initial on a laundry bag – can turn a simple accessory into something very special. Some sewing machines have embroidery programmes. Hand embroidery stitches are always worked from the front of the fabric so you can see the finished effect. With most fabrics, you need to stretch the area you are working on over an embroidery hoop. With an even tension on the fabric, you can then keep an even stitch tension. The weight of the fabric dictates the weight of embroidery thread used. For most purposes stranded embroidery cotton is the ideal choice.

CROSS STITCH

Cross stitch forms the basis of canvaswork embroidery, and is also used on linens and cottons. Working from left to right, make a row of diagonal stitches along the pattern line, taking stitches straight down behind the fabric.

The top stitches must lie at a 45° angle to the fabric weave. Work back along the fabric from right to left, in the same way, taking diagonal stitches over the previous row of stitches. On the back of the fabric, the stitches will again run straight with the fabric grain.

SATIN STITCH

To embroider a design with large areas of colour, use satin stitch (or long and short stitch for very large areas, where satin stitch might pull into loops with wear).

Mark the area to be filled in with a dressmaker's marker or fine basting stitches. Working from the front of the fabric, bring the needle up at one end or at the corner of the shape you are embroidering. Take a stitch across the area, then bring the needle out again on the marked line next to the beginning of the previous stitch. Over large areas, adjust the stitch length, and stagger stitches to prevent a line forming across the embroidery.

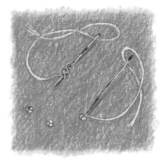

FRENCH KNOTS

French knots are used for spot details, for example the eyes on a face. Bring the needle up through the fabric at the point where you want to make the knot. Take a tiny stitch at the point where the thread comes out of the fabric and, leaving the needle in the fabric, wrap the thread around the point twice. Hold the knot close to the fabric, pull the needle through, then take the needle back through the fabric at the same point, to anchor the knot.

Tip

Always press embroidery and appliqué from the back of the fabric. To avoid crushing the decorative work, cover the ironing board with layers of soft fabric, such as interlining, so that the raised stitching can sink into it.

Facts and figures

CHOOSE TO WORK in either imperial or metric, but do not mix the measurements. For quick reference, a series of conversion charts is given below: detailed conversions of small amounts, fabric yardage/metrage and common fabric widths. These last two charts are for use in stores that sell by the metre when you have worked out quantities in yards.

Fabric lengths

1/8yd	=	10cm
1/4yd	=	20cm
3/8yd	=	40cm
1/2yd	=	45cm
5/8yd	=	60cm
3/4yd	=	70cm
7/8yd	=	80cm
1yd	=	1m
1 1/2yd	=	1.4m
2yd	=	1.9m
2 1/4yd	=	2m
2 1/2yd	=	2.3m
2 3/4yd	=	2.5m
3yd	=	2.7m
3 1/4yd	=	3m
3 1/2yd	=	3.2m
3 3/4yd	=	3.5m
4yd	=	3.7m
4 3/8yd	=	4m
4 1/2yd	=	4.2m
4 7/8yd	=	4.5m
5yd	=	4.6m
5 1/2yd	=	5m
10yd	=	9.2m
10 7/8yd	=	10m
20yd	=	18.5m
21 1/3yd	=	20m

Fabric widths

36in	=	90cm
44/45in	=	115cm
48in	=	120cm
60in	=	150cm

inches / cm·mm scale (0–6 inches / 0–15 cm)

1in = 2.54cm
(2.5cm approx)

1cm = 0.3937in
(3/8in approx)

1ft = 0.3048m

3ft = 1yd = 1m (approx)

1m = 3.281ft

feet / metres scale (0–50 feet / 0–15 metres)

Glossary

Acrylic Synthetic fibre used to make fabric that has similar properties to wool.

Appliqué Method of decorating fabric by stitching on shapes cut from other fabrics.

Basket weave Woven effect in fabric with several strands of warp and weft threads that run together to create a small block effect.

Binding (bias and straight cut) Narrow strips of fabric used to cover the edge of a larger panel of fabric; bias binding is cut diagonally across the fabric (on the bias) so that it can be eased around curves without pleats and puckers.

Bouclé Yarn spun with a loose, looped finish; fabric woven or knitted from bouclé yarn.

Bound button holes Tailored buttonholes finished with strips of fabric binding, rather than with buttonhole stitch.

Braid Woven trimming, used for topstitched decorations on soft furnishings; braids are more substantial, and often more elaborately woven, than ribbons.

Brocade Medium- to heavyweight fabric, woven in two colours to make a satin background with a relief pattern.

Broderie anglaise Cotton fabric that has been pierced and embroidered to create a decorative effect; available as a full-width fabric and as a narrow trim; usually white or cream in colour.

Bump Thick fabric, traditionally a loosely woven brushed cotton, that is used to improve wear of curtains and to give other furnishings a soft and luxurious feel.

Button loops Fabric or hand-stitched loops that act as button holes. Fabric button loops are also known as rouleau loops.

Calico Medium-weight cotton cloth, usually white or unbleached; its low price makes it suitable for making cushion pads with foam or polyester stuffing.

Canopy Fabric suspended over a bed or other feature in a room.

Canvas Heavyweight cotton fabric, often used for deck chair covers.

Canvaswork Embroidery, usually in wool, on special even-weave, holey canvas.

Casing A channel in a piece of fabric made by folding over the top and making two lines of stitching; used to make draw-string bags, fastenings for loose covers, etc.

Check A grid pattern, usually woven but may be printed on to fabric.

Chenille Subtly ribbed, velvety fabric, softer in texture than velvet or corduroy.

Chintz From a Hindu word, chintz is a printed cotton fabric, usually glazed (glossy), but the term is now used to denote any glazed cotton fabric.

Clip To cut into fabric at right angles to the raw edge, or diagonally across corners, to prevent distortion of curved seams and bulk in corners when an item is turned the right side out.

Complementary colours Colours on opposite sides of the colour wheel: red and green; blue and orange; yellow and purple.

Covered buttons Buttons covered with fabric; they can be made with special button forms, available from haberdashery departments and stores.

Crewel work Flowing style of embroidery, developed in 16th-century Europe, usually in wool on linen.

Damask Fabric (usually silk or linen) that has a pattern woven into it; often in a single colour, so that the pattern only shows as the light catches the fabric.

Dobby weave Fabric woven with small, repeating pattern, like a diamond or raised star.

Domette Soft fabric, often synthetic, used as a layer of padding in curtains or under tablecloths.

Dressmaker's carbon paper Paper with coloured coating on the back, so that when you trace an outline on it the motif is transferred to a layer of fabric placed beneath the carbon paper.

Duck Originally used for sails and outerwear, a hard-wearing plain weave fabric in cotton or linen.

Easy-care fabrics Usually woven from a mix of fibres, and requiring minimal ironing.

Electronic sewing machine Electric sewing machine with microchips to make it easy to adjust the type, size and tension of the stitch.

Facing Panel of fabric used to back the main fabric of a cushion or other item around the opening, giving a neat finish.

Faille Silk fabric with a ribbed weave.

Felt A non-woven and non-fraying textile, traditionally in wool, with many craft applications.

Field The background colour of a printed or embroidered piece of fabric.

Fitted sheets Bottom sheets for beds, tailored to fit the mattress, with elasticated corners to hold the sheet taut in place.

Flat seam A simple seam used to join two pieces of fabric with a single line of stitching.

Flat sheet Bed linen that is not fitted at the corners (see Fitted sheets). Often made with a deep hem across the top edge.

French seam Double seam in which the raw edges are completely enclosed.

Geometric print Regular print, of abstract shapes arranged in a regular pattern.

Gingham Lightweight woven fabric, usually white and one other colour, originally a striped fabric, but now used to describe check.

Grain of fabric The lengthways grain is the direction in which the warp threads of the fabric run, parallel to the selvages.

Ground The 'background' fabric used in appliqué, embroidery, etc.

Herringbone A fine, hand-sewn stitch, used to join panels of wadding or to hold hems in place; may also be used as an embroidery stitch.

Housewife pillowcase Pillowcase made with an internal flap at the opening end so that the pillow can be tucked in place.

Interfacing Layer of fabric, often synthetic, non-woven and iron-on, that is used to stiffen lightweight fabrics and make them easier to handle. It may be used to stiffen fabrics used for appliqué motifs.

Interlining Soft fabric (usually domette or bump) used in lined curtains or tablecloths for added weight and luxury.

Jacquard Fabric with colour-woven pattern, similar to brocade or damask, taking its name from the inventor of the loom on which it is woven.

Lapped seam Seam made by overlapping the edges of the panels of fabric to be joined.

Lawn Fine plain-weave cotton fabric.

Layer To trim the seam allowances within a seam to different lengths, thereby eliminating bulk.

Linen union Plain weave fabric made from a mixture of linen and cotton threads.

Lining Layer of fabric added to give improved wear.

Liséré Embroidered and beribboned or elaborately woven fabrics and trimmings.

Mercerized cotton thread Sewing thread specially treated to improve wear and look more lustrous.

Monochromatic scheme Colour scheme that uses only one colour (plus white) in varying tones.

Monotones Scheme using only one tone of a colour.

Motif Abstract or figurative outline or pattern on printed or woven fabric, or pattern used for embroidery, appliqué, etc.

Muslin Fine, loosely woven cotton fabric.

Notch To cut a V-shaped wedge out of the seam allowance; this is done so that pieces of fabric can be matched when they are being stitched together, and also to reduce bulk in curved seams when an item is turned the right side out.

Organdie Fine stiff cotton, open-weave fabric, now often available in synthetic fibres.

Organza Finely woven stiff silk, made from a particular type of twisted silk yarn.

Ottoman A heavy, twill-weave fabric, in silk, linen, cotton or synthetic fibre.

Overlock machine Advanced sewing machine that forms stitches in a more elaborate way than a traditional sewing machine; particularly useful for stretch fabric.

Oxford pillowcase Housewife pillowcase with a wide, flat border all around the edge.

Paisley An intricate pattern with elongated and curved oval motifs, originating in India but taking its name from the Scottish town renowned for its textile industry.

Petit point Fine cross stitch, worked in wool on needlepoint canvas.

Pile The 'fur' of a carpet or of a velvety fabric.

Piqué A light- or medium-weight cotton fabric woven in a single colour with a fine, embossed effect.

Plaid Colour-woven fabric (a check).

Polyester wadding Thick, soft, lightweight padding available in standard widths and thicknesses.

Primary colours The three basic colours – red, blue and yellow – from which all other colours can be mixed (with the addition of black and white).

Provençal print A small, geometric interpretation of paisley patterns, printed in strong colours on lightweight plain-weave cotton.

Pucker Unsightly gathering along a seam line, caused by a blunt needle or a bulky seam.

PVC A plastic coating applied to fabrics to make them waterproof and wipeable.

Rayon A synthetic fibre – the first one to be developed – that imitates silk.

Rouleau A fine tube of fabric, used as fastening or to make button loops.

Ruching Gathering fabric to create a panel of luxurious folds.

Sateen Cotton fabric woven to produce a glossy effect.

Satin A type of weave in which warp threads run over the surface of the fabric to give a glossy finish; a silk fabric with a satin weave.

Satin stitch Closely worked stitch; may be worked in lines by sewing machine or over larger areas by hand.

Scrim Stiff, loosely woven lightweight linen fabric.

Seam allowance The allowance around the edge of a piece of fabric for making a seam. Add a seam allowance to the finished dimensions before cutting out.

Seam line The marked or imaginary line around the edge of a piece of fabric marking the line of stitching when a seam is made.

Seam tape Firmly woven narrow cotton tape used to stop seams distorting; the tape is positioned along the seam line on the wrong side of the fabric, and stitched into the seam as the layers of fabric are joined.

Secondary colours The three colours – purple, green and orange – obtained by mixing any two primary colours.

Seersucker Plain woven fabric, often striped or checked, in which groups of warp and/or weft threads are drawn tighter, creating rows of ruching down or across the fabric.

Selvage The woven, non-fraying edges of a length of fabric.

Serging machine See overlock machine.

Shot silk Silk fabric woven with different colours for the warp and weft, creating a fabric that reflects different shades as it catches the light.

Silk dupion Fabric made from silk spun by a particular type of silkworm: two silkworms spin a double cocoon producing a double thread that can be unravelled for weaving.

Taffeta Plain fabric, usually silk, with a glossy, stiff finish.

Tarlatan Stiffened fabric, similar in weight to muslin.

Tartan Originating in Scotland, tartan is wool fabric woven to create a checked design; each clan or family traditionally had its own particular tartan.

Template A pattern; when cutting repeated identical shapes, for appliqué or patchwork, the template is cut out of stiff card so that it can be used over and over again.

Tertiary colours Colours containing all of the three primary colours.

Thread count The number of threads in a specified area (a square inch) of a woven fabric.

Ticking Tightly woven fabric with a woven stripe; featherproof with black and off-white stripes, but now available in a range of natural and muted colours.

Toile de Jouy Cotton fabric, originating in 18th-century France, with figurative scenes printed in a single colour on a neutral background.

Topstitching A bold line of stitches used to emphasize seams or finish hems.

Touch-and-close fastening Synthetic fastening, made with plastic loops on one half, which link into a furry pile stitched to the opposite side of the opening.

Towelling Woven fabric with a looped pile on both sides.

Trim To cut away excess fabric.

Twill (weave) A weave in which the warp threads form a diagonal rib over the surface of the cloth.

Valance A 'skirt' around a bed, which hides the bed base and legs; a gathered fabric strip across the top of a window treatment, which hides tracks and poles.

Velvet Woven fabric with a pile; may be made from a wide range of fibres.

Voile Translucent fabric made of cotton or synthetic fibre.

Warp The threads that run up and down a woven piece of cloth.

Webbing A broad, woven braid. Traditional hessian webbing or modern rubber webbing is used in upholstery; webbing from synthetic fibres or cotton may be used for straps and ties.

Weft The threads running across a woven piece of cloth.

Yarn Thread (natural or man-made fibre) that has been spun or twisted so that it can be woven or used for embroidery or knitting.

Index

accessories 12
appliqué 46–7
   bed linen 32–3
   sun and moon cot
      quilt 40–5

bag, laundry 48–9
basting, quilts 37
bedcovers 34–5
bias binding 63, 65
binding 63–4
   bound-edged tablecloth
      and napkins 18–19
   mitring corners 64
   quilted comforters 38
   sun and moon cot
      quilt 44
blanket stitch 17
buttonholes 70
buttons, fabric-covered 71

colours 10, 51
comforters, quilted 36–9
cords
   draw-string bags 49
   piping 65–6
corners
   clipping 60
   mitring 62–3, 64, 72
   piping 66
cot quilt 40–5
cotton fabrics 8, 9–10, 27
cross stitch 73
curved seams, clipping
   60
cutlery roll 24–5

draw-string bags 48–9
duvet covers 28–9, 30–1

edgings
   appliqué 32–3
   binding 63–4

table linen 16–17
embroidery 73
enlarging an image 42

fabrics
   bed linen 26–7
   lampshades 50–1
   pattern matching 59
   table linen 8–10, 14
   throws 35
faced hems 63
fastenings 70–1
flat fell seams 61
flat seams 60
flat sheets 29
fleece, padded placemat
   22–3
French knots 73
French seams 61
frills 66–7
fringing 16

hemming stitch 21
hems 15, 21, 62–3
hemstitch 62
herringbone stitch 69
hooks and eyes 70
housewife-style
   pillowcases 31

interfacings 68
interlinings 69
ironing 59

lace edgings 17
lampshades 50–1
   fabric-covered card
      lampshade 56–7
   recovering 54–5
   stiffened silk shade
      52–3
laundry bag 48–9
linen 8, 9, 26–7

lockstitch 69
loops, rouleau 70–1

mats, padded 22–3
measuring up
   bed linen 28
   duvet covers 30
   quilts 37
   tablecloths 15, 20
mitring
   bound corners 64
   hems 62–3
   trimmings 72

napkins 15
   bound-edged 18–19
   edging 16–17

padded placemat 22–3
patchwork, sun and moon
   cot quilt 40–5
pattern pieces 59
patterned fabrics
   lampshades 51
   matching patterns 59
   table linen 10–12
patterns, transferring 33
picnic accessories 24–5
pillowcases 28–9, 31
piping 65–6, 67
placemats, padded 22–3
pleated lampshades 55
press studs 70
pressing 59, 73

quilts
   quilted comforters
      36–9
   sun and moon cot
      quilt 40–5

rouleau loops 70–1
round tablecloths 20–1

satin stitch 16–17, 43, 73
seams 60–1
   pressing 59
   tablecloths 15
sheeting fabric 10, 28
sheets 28–9
stiffening lampshade
   fabric 52–3
sun and moon cot
   quilt 40–5

tablecloths 14–15
   bound-edged tablecloth
      18–19
   edging 16–17
   round tablecloths 20–1
throws 34–5
ties, fabric 71
topstitching 64, 72
   frills 67
   padded placemat 23
touch-and-close
   fastening 70
transferring patterns 33
trimmings
   lampshades 51
   mitring corners 72

valances 29

wadding
   joining 69
   padded placemat 23
   quilted comforters 36

zigzag machine stitch 61
zips 65

Acknowledgements

Photography

Laura Ashley Home Autumn/Winter 2000
Collection 7, 8, 29, 30
Crowson Fabrics 5 top, 49
Dulux 14 top
Elizabeth Whiting Associates 14 bottom, 22, 51 right
Anna French Ltd 4 bottom, 37
Octopus Publishing Group Ltd.
  Rupert Horrox front cover top, back cover centre left, 18, 19, 24, 25, 31, 56
  David Loftus 1 bottom, 3, 4 top, 10 top, 11 top, 11 bottom, 12, 16 left, 16 Right, 17, 23, 35 bottom, 40
  Lucy Mason 9
  Peter Myers 1 top, 5 bottom, 39, 51 left, 57
  David Parmitter back cover top left, 20, 33, 41, 45, 48, 50, 53
  Bill Reavell 2
  Paul Ryan 6, 34, 35 top, 46, 47, 55, 58
  John Sims 10 bottom
  Debi Treloar 13
  Polly Wreford 26
The Interior Archive
  Simon Brown back cover bottom left, 27
  Edina van der Wyck front cover bottom, 28
Sanderson 38, 54

For Hamlyn

Editorial Manager: Jane Birch
Senior Designer: Claire Harvey
Project Manager: Jo Lethaby
Designer: Mark Stevens
Picture Researcher: Christine Junemann
Senior Production Controller: Louise Hall
Illustrator: Jane Hughes